Living Above The Fray

Learning The Seven Healthy Leadership Principles That Will Shelter You From The Destructive Effects Of Leader-I-Tis

A Book Of Leadership Stories And Biblical Principles

For The Quality Leader

Dr. Denny Bates

Living Above The Fray

Living Above The Fray is written as a tool for the people of God to use in order to grow in their faith and then to pass it on to other believers. The purpose of the copyright is to prevent the reproduction, misuse, and abuse of the material. Please address all requests for information or permission to:

Something New Christian Publishers

E-Mail dennybates@gmail.com

On the Web: www.dennybates.com

or visit my teaching blog at

http://thequalitydisciple.blogspot.com

or you can "friend" me on Facebook at
www.facebook.com/denny.bates

or follow me on Twitter @dennybates

What Is The Fray?
A usually disorderly or protracted fight, struggle, or dispute

[6] *In his grace, God has given us different gifts for doing certain things well. So if God has given you the ability to prophesy, speak out with as much faith as God has given you.* [7] *If your gift is serving others, serve them well. If you are a teacher, teach well.* [8] *If your gift is to encourage others, be encouraging. If it is giving, give generously.* **If God has given you leadership ability, take the responsibility seriously.** *And if you have a gift for showing kindness to others, do it gladly.* [9] *Don't just pretend to love others. Really love them. Hate what is wrong. Hold tightly to what is good.* [10] *Love each other with genuine affection, and take delight in honoring each other.* [11] *Never be lazy, but work hard and serve the Lord enthusiastically.* **Romans 12:6-11** *(NLT)*

Paul, the Apostle

The pen is mightier than the sword.

Edward Bulwer-Lytton

Dedicated To My Mentors

To Dr. Morris Anderson, Mr. Knox Sherer,

Dr. Rick Higgins, Dr. Al McKechnie

"For in the abundance of counselors there is victory"

Foreword

I have been granted two privileges in relation to writing this foreword. One is the opportunity to read this book before anyone else, allowing me a bit of a head start in applying the Biblical principles of leadership conveyed on the following pages. The other, more personal, privilege is the opportunity to know the author and count him as a friend. It is through that friendship that I have been able to witness (for nearly two decades) Denny Bates' life journey—both among and above the fray. His life, like each of our own, has provided clear opportunities to experience both perspectives. As he outlines in this book, Dr. Bates has harvested valuable lessons from his personal and professional experiences, and he offers them here in a manner that holds benefit for each of us.

The lessons outlined on the subsequent pages are rooted in Biblical principle, but they have a profoundly personal feel. The simple test for the reader is to find yourself in this book. Where are you? On what page? In what passage? Keep in mind that you are reading this book for a reason—not just to avoid succumbing to Leader-I-Tis (as Dr. Bates terms it) but to begin to thrive as an effective leader. This book is about the personal accumulation of experience, but it is also a story of transcendence. It is about moving beyond your present circumstances to more fully realize your leadership potential. I encourage you to find yourself in the pages, the stories, and the lessons that follow. Allow yourself the chance to rise above your circumstances and live, whenever possible, *above the fray.*

In essence, this book is a mirror reflection for us all in regard to our leadership potential—and the challenges we face in seeking to fulfill that potential. The examples that are offered in this book remind us first to see ourselves in the reality of our circumstances. Yet we are also reminded that we hold the power—through faith—to change those circumstances via a more purposeful pursuit of our potential. We must, as Dr. Bates instructs, be faithful and do the work that God has called and equipped us to do. We must be purposeful in our actions, but we must also be mindful of the guidance that is available to us, both through our own experience and through Christian teaching, that enables us to meet our potential as leaders of faith.

As you explore the seven Biblical principles for living above the fray, I encourage you to be purposeful in your self-reflection. Open your mind to seeing yourself in the midst of the fray (as many of us often are) and then find the path to living above the fray (as all of us can do). It is through such faithful self-reflection and focused action that each of us can achieve our full potential as leaders. ~ *Dr. Lee Pearson*

BOOK OUTLINE

Foreword: Dr. Lee Pearson vi

PART ONE: A LEADERSHIP STORY

Prelude: Leader-I-Tis 1

    The Definition 4

    A Case Study 4

    Twelve Leadership Failures That Will Sink An
    Organization 9

    The Early Symptoms 12

Introduction 17

Back To The Boardroom: We Are Stuck. Now What? 20

PART TWO: A BIBLICAL RESPONSE FOR LIVING ABOVE THE FRAY

Leadership Principle One ~ Stay Useful! Living Above
The Fray Begins Here*: We Need To Be Clean And Useful (2
Timothy 2:20-21)* 43

Leadership Principle Two ~ Stay Strategic!

Living Above The Fray Means We Are Intentional In Actions
and In Right Relationships*: We Need To Be Purposeful In What
We Pursue And With Whom We Pursue It (2 Timothy 2:22)* . . .52

Leadership Principle Three ~ Stay Alert!

Living Above The Fray Insists We Exhibit Excellent People Skills: *We Need To Learn How To Effectively Relate To Difficult People (2 Timothy 2:23-26)* 60

Leadership Principle Four ~ Stay Strong!

Living Above The Fray Means We Refuse To Sink To The Level Of Those Who Sin Against Us: *We Need To Beware Of The People Who Are Bullies (2 Timothy 3:1-9)* 68

Leadership Principle Five ~ Stay Connected!

Living Above The Fray Requires Good Mentors: *We Need To Seek Out The Kinds Of Leaders Who Live Out What They Teach And Believe And Follow Their Example (2 Timothy 3:10-15)* . . 82

Leadership Principle Six ~ Stay Grounded!

Living Above The Fray Is Fueled By The Study Of And The Personal Application Of The Bible: *We Need To Embrace The Word Of God As Our Guide So We May Faithfully Live Out The Christian Life (2 Timothy 3:16-17)* 96

Leadership Principle Seven ~ Stay Focused!

Living Above The Fray Means We Keep The Main Thing, The Main Thing: *We Need To Be Faithful And Do What God Has Called And Equipped Us To Do For Him (2 Timothy 4:1-5)* 109

Epilogue: Revisiting The Boardroom 139

Subject Index 142

Scripture Index 164

How You Can Have A Relationship With Jesus 166

Bibliography 168

Resources 175

Quality Leadership Consultants 177

Something New Ministries 181

What Others Are Saying About Dr. Denny Bates 182

Praise For Living Above The Fray 186

About The Author 189

Prelude:

Let me tell you a story about what it is like *to live in the fray* and learn *how to live above the fray*. In a "perfect world" (yeah, right), we would work in environments of grace where everything that affected us went our way. We want be treated fairly. We want to be honored. We want to be considered as valuable by the organization. We want others to understand us just as we want to understand others. We want to expect all of this, and so much more. And we would be kidding ourselves, wouldn't we? Remember, we are not in a perfect world. No perfect organization, no perfect family, no perfect business, no perfect church, and most certainly, no perfect Christian. One of the distinguishing marks of an effective leader is to be able to lead when things are not going his or her way. An effective leader still leads even though he or she is not treated fairly. A gifted leader leads without having to be honored by his or her superiors and peers. A leader who is secure in his or her skin is able to lead (and bear fruit) in spite of others who either refuse to lead or are incapable of leading. A secure leader presses on, even in the midst of the most challenging of circumstances. How important is leadership? Leadership specialist John Maxwell states that everything rises and falls on leadership. Most anyone can lead if the circumstances are easy. But what are we to do when we serve in an unhealthy environment? This much is true: it is during the most challenging of times where we experience our greatest growth as a leader. Do the biblical principles of leadership "work" while we are in the fray? Check out this dysfunctional leadership team and see if any part of this story resonates with your experience.

PART ONE: A LEADERSHIP STORY

You can't depend on your eyes when your imagination is out of focus.

Mark Twain

Ten Angry Men

A Case Study of Leaders Who Were Infected by Leader-I-Tis
And How They Caused Great Harm to Their Organization

LEADER-I-TIS

What is it?

Leader-I-Tis is a horrible disease that attacks once healthy organizations and severely impairs them, rendering them mostly ineffective and impotent. Leader-I-Tis is the leading cause of broken relationships and the killing of vision in an organization. Highly contagious, those without a strong backbone are highly susceptible to infection. If detected early, there is a cure that may save the organization from irrelevance. If Leader-I-Tis is ignored and rationalized away, a slow and painful death of the organization is the certain outcome.

Ten men, all good (at least most of them were) men, sat around the conference table. Representing a wide array of education and life experience, each man had a unique role to play in the organization. Some of these men were highly skilled in domestic affairs and a few others had vast international experience. Each of the men was well respected in their various fields of expertise, boasting of professional resumes that many would define as personal success stories. Some of these men had the privilege of being on the ground floor when the organization was formed. Yes, those were the

4

days of humble and meager times. There was a certain kind of purity, a noble and just cause, in coming up with the idea that years later would benefit many others. Like all other organizations, people come and go. Years into the life of the organization, others were added to the governing board of leaders. This came after a careful screening to make sure everyone was on the same page. But like trying to herd cats, some new members of the governing board did not see eye to eye on everything with the original founders when it came to "the company line." Instead of being "Yes" men, they began to raise what were unspeakable questions (at least in the minds of the organization's founders and their adherents). Though it pained them to do so, a few of these new leaders began to ask some hard questions. In doing so, the room became tense.

As one would gaze around the room, the face of each man tells a fascinating story. One man left behind a promising career and took a job that paid far less. He was the silent type, but had a lot to say if only his peers around the table would hear his heart. Sitting across him was a man who has never changed jobs as an adult. Also the quiet type, he rarely spoke up during their meetings. Sad. He also could contribute a wealth of deep wisdom to the group, if only he could muster up the courage and speak up. Sitting next to the head of the board chairman was a man who simply wanted to please those who had the most power in the room. The years seem to have quickly swept by in this man's life and still today he does not know who he really is. To his frustration, no matter how hard he tries to put on his suit he feels empty. He wants to be like his heroes, but in truth, he really secretly wants to be his own man, whoever that is. He is still waiting to find out who that man really is.

In the room was a man who was torn. Truly, he wanted to do the right thing and live by the right principle; but could he afford the cost of losing the respect of the power brokers of the group? Like an acrobat walking on a tight rope, this man sought to do the same. It was a dangerous stunt, knowing that there was no net below. Also in the room was a tall man who seemed to never raise the level of his voice. This man also lived in the shadows of the strong ones in the room, always deferring to the ones who talked louder than he did. Sitting next to him, was the energetic one, and the short one. He did a lot of talking but those who knew him best secretly knew that he was all that— just talk. Being a favorite of the most powerful man in the room gave him access into the inner sanctums of power. Sitting across from him was a man who was in competition for having the gentlest spirit in the room. He always came to the meetings prepared to contribute, but as much as he sought to convince the others of the rightness of his point, the keepers of the power treated him like an outcast. After enough of these confrontations, he simply gave up and gave in and willingly became another member of the silent majority.

The most powerful man in the room was shielded by two others. One of the protectors of the most powerful man in the room spoke softly, but carried a big stick. The group knew the rules: when he spoke, the group agreed with whatever he said. And strangely so, whatever he said always supported the most powerful man in the room. The other protector was never a really good leader, but he made an excellent follower. He was ready and willing to do or say whatever the most powerful man in the room desired. And what made the most powerful man in the room the most powerful man in the room? He was the one who talked the loudest. And when he talked and scowled at the same time, the weak in heart cowered and ran for cover.

Over the years the times, challenges, and people changed. But what did not change was the culture of the organization and the dysfunction and co-dependency of the leadership team. In a very weird kind of way, they needed each other's dysfunction, which fed their own. Instead of adapting to the changes, the leaders of the organization hunkered down into denial mode and quickly got left behind. Every organization's life cycle has a peak. If the necessary adjustments in vision and methodology are not made in time, the weight and gravity of a negative momentum picks up steam and is rarely fixable. When history presented to these leaders an opportunity to lead and to lead well, each man contributed to the failure of the organization. And as the downward spiral of the organizational health picked up speed, the more frustrated each one became. Why were they so frustrated? They were losing control of the organization and their people. Every countermeasure they tried failed to stop the hemorrhaging as talented and highly valued support people left the organization in droves. Tragically, they were killing the very thing they were trying to save. Blaming others for the failure of the organization, they retreated into their alternative reality. Call it stubbornness. Call it ignorance. Call it pride. Call it a failure to take an introspective look in the mirror. If only they had known about the twelve leadership failures that sink an organization.

Twelve Leadership Failures That Will
Sink An Organization

(1) A Failure To Lead By Example

Are the leaders willing to do what they are asking others to do?

Are the leaders willing to show others how to succeed?

(2) A Failure To Create A Safe Place For Discussion

Are the leaders willing to be approachable and listen?

Are the leaders willing to accept constructive criticism from others?

(3) A Failure To Plan For The Future

Are the leaders willing to be forward thinking when met with a challenge or problem, rather than taking the attitude "we've always done it this way before?"

Are the leaders willing to set strategic, measurable goals for the organization's health?

(4) A Failure To Learn From The Past

Are the leaders willing to express humility when things have not gone as planned?

Are the leaders willing to make the necessary changes so that history will not repeat itself?

(5) A Failure To Invest In Future Leaders

Are the leaders willing to become mentors to the next generation of leadership?

Are the leaders willing to pass the baton of leadership and not grip power until the bitter end?

(6) A Failure To Appreciate And Praise Others In The Organization's Successes

Are the leaders willing to share the glory when things are going well?

Are the leaders willing to promote the contributions of those who serve behind the scenes?

(7) A Failure To Distinguish The Difference Between Managing Programs And Leading People

Are leaders willing to care more about building a

relationship with people rather than simply trying to manage them?

Are leaders willing to make people feel important?

(8) A Failure To Empower Members To Reach Their Full Potential

Are leaders willing to make a concerted effort to lead others towards growth?

Are leaders willing to be replaced by those they have empowered to grow?

(9) A Failure To Communicate In A Clear And Convincing Way

Are leaders willing to make sure that communication is clear and consistent?

Are leaders willing to listen and learn from others?

(10) A Failure To Capture The Moment And Build Upon Energy And Momentum

Are leaders willing to lead on the cutting edge of change?

Are leaders willing to spend the necessary resources

to ensure momentum does not fade away?

(11) A Failure To Build A Team That Has Great Chemistry

Are leaders willing to make the necessary investment of time to make sure "the right people are on the bus?"

Are leaders willing to do what is necessary in order to build a team building culture in the organization?

(12) A Failure To Make Strategic Adjustments During An Historic Challenge

Are leaders willing to think outside the box in order to compensate for a change in culture or circumstances?

Are leaders willing to admit incorrect assumptions and adjust to a new strategy that may demand structural changes in how the organization operates?

On The Edge Of Leader-I-Tis: What are the early symptoms?

One of the great ironies of Leader-I-Tis is that a leader can lead well in one organization but become sick and irrelevant in another. I suppose there are several theories out there, but maybe it all leads back to one's "calling." There are some leaders who are placed in positions of leadership, not because of a "call" or due to an extraordinary skill, but because of popularity, because of politics, because of a desire by the other leaders to gather like-minded leaders who will buy into the organization's culture. It is within this closed group where the seeds of elitism and entitlement ferment and grow. Unseen by most of the organization's members, the leaders become intoxicated with the power of leadership and, without realizing it, have begun to infect themselves with Leader-I-Tis. Once the infection spreads into the members of the organization, it becomes a plague, putting all who come into contact with the organization at risk.

One of the early symptoms of Leader-I-Tis is a growing separation from the members of the organization who connect with the outside world. In a business, this would be the customer. In a non-profit, this would be a donor and the recipients of the services rendered. An air of superiority, a sense of being better than, will evolve into a more serious circumstance that, if unchecked, will lead to a full-blown case of Leader-I-Tis.

Another early symptom of Leader-I-Tis is a fear to change the status quo. In the case of an organization, there can be a fear of replacing old ideas with new ideas, replacing old leaders with new ones. Though cast as a legitimate concern (what will happen if the new leaders are not as good as we are?), refusal to create a culture of leadership transition will cripple an organization. History is full of examples of leaders who passed on the baton, the mantle of leadership to others (Moses to Joshua; Elijah to Elisha; Paul to Timothy, etc.). History is also filled with negative examples of those leaders who did not pass on leadership to future leaders. Some of these organizations, built upon the personality of one leader, were never the same again. Others simply died.

A familiar, and all too common, early symptom is a lack of commitment of the leadership to take on the monumental, defining issues of an organization. There are many reasons why the hard things are ignored and left undone. One reason is simple: some leaders are just tired. They are tired physically. They are tired emotionally. They are tired mentally. They are tired and do not have the energy or desire to tackle the hard cases. For them, it is much easier for them to justify why they cannot act. For many, they feel they have put in their time and now have earned the right to coast. Others may see the need for change, but in their own mind, have raised the white flag of surrender. They do not have the heart to fight for the cause. So, they stay silent and submit to the whims of others. Another reason for why leaders refuse to face the hard leadership decisions is a paralyzing one: personal fear. Fear to act. Fear to lead. Fear to change. Fear is the cancer that eats a leader alive. Instead of being agents of change, the fear-struck leader goes into personal survival mode and neglects his or her duties for caring for the organization.

This leads to another early sign that Leader-I-Tis is lurking right under the surface. There are some leaders who lead, not out of courage and boldness, but out of fear *and* intimidation. These leaders are afraid of the stronger personality in the room (the one who yells loudest with words or with body language or both). Instead of standing by one's convictions, these timid leaders seek to avoid conflict at all cost. It does not matter to them what they feel in their heart. What matters to them is not to rock the boat but urgently seek to just get along and not be yelled at by the leader. At the core of their being they want to be accepted and made a part of the elitist club within the organization (even if it means losing all dignity and self-respect). Leader-I-Tis, in its beginning stages sears the conscience. It is a wound that cannot be seen by others on one's skin. No, it is far deeper and more damaging than that. Instead, the germ of Leader-I-Tis is aggressive and can forever change the personality, the destiny and well being of the stricken leader.

Leader-I-Tis grows in an organization when personalities become more important than the greater good of the organization. A self-serving culture is formed where the organization is designed to meet the needs of its leaders instead of the leaders meeting the needs of the organization. Instead of servant leadership being the expectation of every leader, the organization's leaders live a life of self-entitlement. It is this sense of entitlement from leaders with Leader-I-Tis that drains the very life out of the organization.

So, you may ask, what does all of this have to do with me and, perhaps, even you? This book is my story. It might be your story too. If you have lived and experienced any of this, you may feel trapped and doomed to a life of mediocrity and personal defeat. Or, possibly, you are willing to take the necessary steps towards wholeness. This book will be your guide in helping you live above the fray. I invite you to take this journey with me and with a host of others who have discovered the path to the greatest freedom you will ever experience: to survive a toxic, unhealthy, environment and come out even stronger—all because of the goodness, mercy, and grace of God.

Introduction:

This is the question I am proposing to you: In a toxic organizational culture is it possible for you to survive (and perhaps even, to an extent, thrive) while serving in an organization where a dysfunctional leadership team cultivates and protects a personality cult that makes everyone sick, and maybe, even you? In this organization you are overlooked, marginalized, bullied, demeaned, quenched, made to question your own heart (*are my motives pure?*), made to question your own mind (*am I the insane one and the inmates are right?*), made to question your ability to hear God's voice on your own (*am I not as spiritual or wise as the leaders who insist they are more wise and more spiritual?*), discouraged, in the throes of depression AND YET, somehow, someway, you get over to the other side where you find yourself stronger, not weaker; better, not bitter; and more convinced than ever before that nothing in your experience can afford to be wasted. The hurt, the disappointment, and the death of precious dreams can lead to an even greater outcome. Now, finally, you have something to say that will have value to others who have also suffered and perhaps have yet to find any comfort or meaning in their pain.

I have been writing this book for years. My source material has literally taken over thirty years to accumulate, process and apply to my life. There have been some good times and lots of challenging ones too. By the grace of God I can call myself a survivor. I began my journey of faith working for communities of faith. Idealistic was I. Naïve, of course. I trusted that those in leadership always had my best interest in mind. Sure I did. Most of you have too. If you have experienced spiritual abuse and neglect from church and ministry leaders and want some answers concerning the questions *how it happened to you, why it happened to you, and how God can bring good out of it,* this book is written for your encouragement.

In theory we "should" expect certain things out of certain people and organizations, especially when the people profess to be followers of Jesus and the organization is a church or mission agency. But we often forget that people, even Christians, don't always love in the way that Christ has taught us to love. We forget that egos, unsubmitted to the Lordship of Jesus, can be as large as Mount Everest and bring great harm and devastating damage to the individual and the cause of Christ. This book is a story of great pain and an even greater gain. It is a story of spiritual abuse and spiritual abundance. More than anything, this is a story of how a person can experience such negative circumstances and at the end of the day have such a wonderful testimony of the goodness and kindness of God, bitter-free, and formed in the character of Christ. My hope and prayer for you is that you will join the ranks of the many "wounded healers" who are striving to make an eternal difference, living above the fray.

In His grip,

Dr. Denny Bates

Winter, 2013

Back To The Boardroom:
We Are Stuck. Now What?

The culture of the leadership group for years was to deny all responsibility and blame shift the organization's challenges to certain employees or disgruntled customers. This strategy seemed to be working until the truth of the problem became apparent to some of the board members. Of course, these were not the gatekeepers of the power, but nonetheless, they felt it was long past time to share their concerns with the rest of the board.

In what was a modern-day parting of the Red Sea the powerbrokers decided to allow a leadership consultant give to the board, select employees and customers an assessment. He was known for his ability to shoot straight. How did this consultant make it through a divided board? The ones who sat in the powerful seats thought they were hiring another yes man. In addition, some of the guys with the big, intimidating sticks were absent from the meeting. Thus, the motion to hire the consultant was made and seconded and voted for by a five to two vote. The ayes have it and the meticulous work of looking beneath the surface began.

Dr. Davis had lived long enough to see about everything one could experience as a leadership specialist. He had leadership experience in a variety of settings, in both non-profit organizations as well as market place companies. But no matter the context, he came to discover that principles are principles and are applicable and true in every organization. As Dr. Davis studied different organizations, he sought the answer to why once healthy organizations became sick. Disturbing him even deeper was of these same sick organizations he studied not only did the leaders deny they were sick but saw any kind of critique as a personal attack and betrayal.

Davis concluded that there are at least twelve leadership failures that will sink and destroy an organization. Armed with this knowledge, he began to make personal appointments with each board member. Interviewing each board member, he sought to record, in their own words, where each one stood on why the organization was struggling. Surprisingly, in spite of being confronted with the facts on the ground, some of these leaders remained in denial mode and even questioned the agenda of Dr. Davis. Such is the life reality of the leadership specialist. Underappreciated at best. At worst completely ignored.

Tony was first up on Dr. Davis' list to question. Tony had owned at one time his own business and served on the boards of companies and ministries. One day Tony sold his business and took a leap of faith in his new endeavor. Tony is the guy who wants to make a difference in his world. His challenge was to make a difference on this board and in this organization. The first question Dr. Davis posed to Tony was this: "Tony, why do you feel so powerless to turn this ship around?" Tony thought about it and simply stated, "I've been thinking about it a lot lately. I'm going to wait it out and hope that things will eventually change for the good. Patience is a great virtue, you know." Dr. Davis listened with interest and after hearing Tony's response recorded this in his notebook: "Tony's leadership strategy is based upon hope as in hope the organizational problems go away on their own."

One of the malicious techniques of Leader-I-Tis is how it numbs normally good leaders into a stupor. Tony has the reputation of being a world-class businessman, but in this case the epidemic of Leader-I-Tis in this organization made him ill. After Dr. Davis' interview with Tony was over and Tony had left the room, he thought to himself: "Sick leaders cannot make sick organizations well." Davis is right. Tony's approach was "Que sera sera, what ever will be will be." His "hope" for change spiraled into "nope" for change. Why? Tony failed miserably when it came to the twelfth leadership failure. It is . . .

#12: A Failure To Make Strategic Adjustments During An Historic Challenge

Are leaders willing to think outside the box in order to compensate for a change in culture or circumstances?

Are leaders willing to admit incorrect assumptions and adjust to a new strategy that may demand structural changes in how the organization operates?

After Tony, Carl was the next person Dr. Davis interviewed. His friends called him "steady Carl." Carl never changed jobs, he never changed his wife, and he never changed his outward emotion. He also never changed what he shared at the board meetings: little, to nothing. It wasn't like Carl was not sharp. He had a good perspective on life and business. The only problem was no one ever asked him his opinion. That is the life of the introvert. We tend to be quiet, very quite people. Dr. Davis picked up on this quirk of personality really quick and asked Carl, "Why don't you speak up? You are a full-fledged member of the board. Your organization is leaking employees and customers like a sieve and you say nothing. What is that about Carl?"

Carl had an answer, a really good one in fact but he dare not let it move across his lips. In his mind he knew the reason: he feared his ideas would be rejected and, in a really perverted way of thinking, they would be rejecting him too. For Carl, it was not worth the risk. Carl's approach to his leadership challenge and his failure to lead well sickened him with Leader-I-Tis. Why did he get ill? He not only failed to communicate out of his own insecurity and fear, he failed to communicate in a clear and convincing way.

Leadership Failure #9: A Failure To Communicate In A Clear And Convincing Way

Are leaders willing to make sure that communication is clear and consistent?

Are leaders willing to listen and learn from others?

Waiting for his turn to see Dr. Davis, Mike was the "suit" in the bunch. He really enjoyed fine clothes for two reasons. One, he loved to be seen and admired as the stylish one and two (and this was his secret), he was able to hide in his costume of perceived self-confidence and success. Inside his head was a completely different landscape. Dr. Davis had his suspicions that all was not on the level with Mike. He talked the good talk, but seemed to lack substance. It reminded him of what one of his mentors told him a long time ago: the proof is always in the pudding. In Mike's case, his interview proved to Dr. Davis that Mike had no clue who he was, nor did he care to know. He just wanted to be like the boss and he was willing to do that even if it meant losing himself in the process.

Dr. Davis started Mike's interview with this question: "Given the fact that your organization is sick and is losing employees and clients, are you opposed to introducing new ideas and new leaders in the organization?" It did not take Mike long to respond, much to Dr. Davis' chagrin. "I believe that the problem is not with us but with them. We are relieved that they have left. We are much better off now with a committed core than with unloyal employees and clients who were not on board with our mission. Yes, I realize that many have left for "so called" better opportunities, but we are not going to change a thing. We are going to hunker down and keep on doing those things that made us great."

Dr. Davis interrupted and said, "So, you are not wiling to change your methodology in order to regain your market share as well as seek to retain both customers and employees?" "Exactly. We are going to remain the same. We will not and do not need to change anything." Dr. Davis was surprised, but not so surprised by this unwillingness to admit the need to change. Mike had become one of the sicker ones with Leader-I-Tis. If fact, he was so infected with it, he became a willing carrier and infected innocent people. Leader-I-Tis has a way of doing that when a leader fails to plan for the future.

Leadership Failure #3: A Failure To Plan For The Future

Are the leaders willing to be forward thinking when met with a challenge or problem, rather than taking the attitude "we've always done it this way before?"

Are the leaders willing to set strategic, measurable goals for the organization's health?

Three interviews down, only SEVEN more to go, Dr. Davis noted. The next man on deck intrigued Dr. Davis. Joe had a pretty impressive life resume. He had visited many countries and lived in one outside of America for a while too. Here is one of the sad things about Joe. He did not have to impress anyone with who he was, what he knew, and what he experienced—but *he did need to impress others—desperately.* Joe is what is known as a "people pleaser." Joe had a desperate need to be liked, especially by the most important people (at least by the world's standards) in the room. Some call it being a suck up, others just call it sad and pathetic.

Dr. Davis posed this question to Joe and the response somewhat surprised him. "Joe, you are one of the board members in this organization as well as an employee of the organization. Do you think you have an unfair advantage over the other department heads because of your dual positions?" Joe thought about it and cut right to the chase. "I think I am more valuable to the other employees by having a seat on this board. I can be their voice." "But are you really," Dr. Davis inquired. "I have heard from some of the employees that you are protecting your back and not theirs. In fact, if push came to shove they feel certain that you would protect yourself at all cost, and leave them hanging." Joe shot back: "Dr. Davis, you don't understand our culture here. We all work as a team."

After a pregnant pause, Dr. Davis mentioned this nugget of truth. "It's come to my attention that you apologized to a former employee for allowing the board to set him up for failure. With that same employee you had the opportunity to protect a few years later, but due to your incessant need to be liked by those in power, you threw him under the bus." The truth hurts. But an even greater pain occurs when leaders who have all of the power remain in their own protected silos and leave other teammates with less power to fend for themselves. God help them, and God help Joe too. Joe has a serious case of Leader-I-Tis. His failure to build a team that has great chemistry has brought hurt to others.

Leadership Failure #11: A Failure To Build A Team That Has Great Chemistry

Are leaders willing to make the necessary investment of time to make sure "the right people are on the bus?"

Are leaders willing to do what is necessary in order to build a team building culture in the organization?

The interviews continued when Donald came into the room. This was a man that Dr. Davis looked up too. He had to since Donald was a foot taller than Dr. Davis. But Donald's stature was greatly diminished when Dr. Davis discovered that this gentle giant had no backbone for leadership on this board. The paradox really intrigued Dr. Davis. At his other job as a foreman, Donald managed people and he managed them well. But here, it was such a different story. This is why. Donald was a pretty good manager, but a horrible leader. He knew how to manage people but not lead them. On his other job he knew how to move them, but here he failed to motivate them. Donald's experience is no different than what occurs in many organizations. People are treated as "parts," disposed of when they wear out and removed with no rhyme or reason when the organization wants to "go in another direction."

Mostly due to his personality, Donald was more

concerned about not making waves. A leader in this organization, he viewed the program as more important than the people. He was a manager, not a leader and in this case, a failure. He failed to distinguish the difference between managing programs and leading people.

> **Leadership Failure #7: A Failure To Distinguish The Difference Between Managing Programs And Leading People**

Are leaders willing to care more about building a relationship with people rather than simply trying to manage them?

Are leaders willing to make people feel important?

Alan is a pretty funny guy. He always lights up any party he attends. He brings smiles to lots of people, especially to the leaders of his board. He is the court jester. Entertaining yes, but taken seriously? Not a chance. But because he is beloved by the powerful people on the board he is treated as if he really does matter.

Alan's interview with Dr. Davis began with this question: "Alan, tell me about how you view the employees of your company who do the "grunt" work." "The way I see it," Alan replied, "is everyone's got to pay their dues. I paid mine and now that I've got a leadership title on this board I expect everyone to jump when I say jump. I just think I'm entitled because of where I've started." Dr. Davis led with this question: "Share an example with me of why you feel you are entitled to pass on the servant jobs to others." "Sure," Alan said. "In our company we have this meeting room which requires a lot of set up between meetings. When I was younger, I moved a lot of chairs. Now, its time to pass that blessing on to someone else." "Did anyone ever challenge you . . . push back at you?" "Yeah, one guy did, but I put him in his place really quick. 'I'm the boss and you're not, so get to work on those chairs.'"

In this organization, for Alan, it was all about him and the other ones who held the seats of power. Alan committed one of the cardinal sins of Leader-I-Tis: He failed to lead by example.

Leadership Failure #1: A Failure To Lead By Example

Are the leaders willing to do what they are asking others to do?

Are the leaders willing to show others how to succeed?

Dr. Davis welcomed Maurice to the interview room. This might have been his favorite personality. Maurice seemed to be a warm, kind soul. His smile lit up the room as soon as he came in. But the smile soon faded as Dr. Davis began to probe into Maurice's psyche. It seems that Maurice had a history with the leader of the organization. Both were from the same small community and each had worked for the same organization. Maurice's brother also worked there and was the victim of workplace bullying by the same leader. The same leader who had a documented history of this kind of abuse became the leader of a new organization in a new city. Maurice joined him a few years later.

Some things never change. This is true. Sometimes things do change and become even worse. This was also true in the new organization where both men served on the board of leaders. Maurice would hear stories of abuse that would shame him to silence. He knew it was wrong but did not have the courage to speak out and risk becoming the new target for the serial abuser. After hearing his story, Dr. Davis came to this correct conclusion. Even nice guys can get sick from Leader-I-Tis. Maurice failed to learn from the past and in doing so, the abuser continue to abuse, with the permission of the board.

Leadership Failure #4: A Failure To Learn From The Past

Are the leaders willing to express humility when things have not gone as planned?

Are the leaders willing to make the necessary changes so that history will not repeat itself?

31

Dr. Davis glanced at his watch. It was an interesting period of time. Over the course of these first seven interviews his suspicions had been correct: Leader-I-Tis had gone from the early symptoms to a full-blown pandemic. Could it get any worse? Yes, it could and yes it did. Next up were the three most powerful men in the room. Instead of one on one interviews, Dr. Davis decided to do a group session with Dick, Victor, and Aaron—the three most dysfunctional men in the room, but the ones who held power over the others.

Dr. Davis began the interview this way: "After interviewing a select number of your employees and customers, I do have some serious concerns about your leadership style. I'm going to list them for you and then I'd like to hear your perspective before I make my final recommendations to you and to your leadership team. First of all, the feedback I am getting from your employees and customers is they do not feel safe with you. By that I mean, when they seek to offer constructive feedback, you see it as criticism and shut down dissenting voices. Instead of taking a listening posture, you have instead called them un-loyal and malicious gossips. Help me understand the disconnect between you and them. Dick, you can answer first." Remember, Dick is the one everyone listens to. He speaks softly but carries the big stick. On the surface, he is a caring individual until you dig a little bit deeper where you discover that he only cares about protecting "the man." At all costs, even at the cost of slowly destroying the organization, he is committed to overlook the lethal leadership flaws of the main guy. Somehow, Dick has not only assisted in making the toxic Kool-Aid, but is quick to dispense it to anyone who pledges to be a loyal member of the organization.

"Dr. Davis," Dick replied, "We see it quite differently than you do. We hold up the virtue of loyalty as one of our most important core tenants. We feel if our employees and disgruntled customers focus on the negative things, it will divert our attention away from all of the great and positive things that are happening in our organization. It may seem harsh to you, but we are glad to let the naysayers go someplace else. We think of it as pruning off the dead branches so the healthy ones can bear even more fruit."

Dr. Davis paused, took a breath, and pulled out his summary sheet from previous interviews and read it out loud to Dick, Victor, and Aaron. "People do not feel safe with the leadership. They have difficulty trusting anyone in leadership." After taking a sip of water, Dr. Davis went on to say; "I find it sad and disturbing that you have catalogued positive feedback as a negative attack upon you and ultimately upon your organization. You give the outward appearance of being very open to hear the concerns of your employees and customers. But in reality, you have forever shut the door of trust and safety. They no longer trust you and they sure do not feel safe around you. You have not only killed the messenger, you have killed the organization. You have perpetuated one of the worst failures of Leader-I-Tis. You have failed to create a safe place for discussion. "

Leadership Failure #2: A Failure To Create A Safe Place For Discussion

Are the leaders willing to be approachable and listen?

Are the leaders willing to accept constructive criticism from others?

Dr. Davis continued to probe into the thoughts of these powerful leaders who had infected the entire organization and many of its customers with Leader-I-Tis. "Victor, let me address the next question to you." Victor is the consummate "yes man." When he is walking in the shadow of leaders who are more powerful than he, Victor always bends his knee to the will and opinion of those men. It has been said of him that he never created an original thought in his mind. The ideas of those in power were enough original thinking for Victor.

Dr. Davis asked, "Why have you and your leadership

team failed to mentor up-and-coming leaders who show so much promise? You have some gifted employees who feel they have hit the proverbial glass ceiling and will never be able to aspire to the place where you and the other board members sit. What do you say to them, to those who want to rise up in the leadership ranks too?"

Victor looked confused, as if he had never even considered that question. He snapped, "Every board member has earned his seat, and for that matter we believe in lifetime appointments, and none of us are planning on dying any time soon. We are sure not going to step down and take the risk on someone who could never protect the organization as we do." This response grieved Dr. Davis. His grief was not about the intoxicating pride of Victor and his like, but upon the failed opportunity to grow the next generation of leaders.

This is one of the most selfish and shortsighted forms of Leader-I-Tis. It is not only a failure to invest in an organization's greatest human assets but it is also a failure to train and empower the members of the organization to reach their full potential. Combined, these two failures will kill an organization every time.

Leadership Failure #5: A Failure To Invest In Future Leaders

Are the leaders willing to become mentors to the next generation of leadership?

Are the leaders willing to pass the baton of leadership and not grip power until the bitter end?

Leadership Failure #8: A Failure To Empower Members To Reach Their Full Potential

Are leaders willing to make a concerted effort to lead others towards growth?

Are leaders willing to be replaced by those they have empowered to grow?

The final question went to Aaron. "Why do secure people make you so insecure?" Aaron was the guy to whom everyone answered. Some loved him, others feared him; all knew him as the leader who always got what he wanted. Many members of his board learned really quickly that if you crossed him one time, you were put on his "do not like" list resulting in the worst punishment of all for these board members: to be placed outside the inner circle of power and prestige. He was the founding member of the board and lived an entitled life because, obviously, he deserved it.

Aaron believed, as did many others in the organization that everything revolved around him. The organization bowed to his wish one day and gave him a special parking place in the organization's parking lot. They did not stop there. They gave his wife one too. Talk about a sense of entitlement coming in pairs. One night an employee had the audacity to park in her spot. Instead of taking the mature posture, she flew off the handle (maybe it was a broom) and embarrassed herself. (No, wait a minute. People who think it's all about them find it impossible to embarrass themselves.) But she did embarrass others including one of the leaders of the board who saw the whole thing go down, nervously laughed it off, and walked away.

Aaron and his wife are narcissistic leaders. This means all attention, especially the flattering kind, is to be showered upon them. Anything or anyone who seeks to compete with them quickly finds himself or herself under vicious attack. The motto of Aaron and his wife is blunt and to the point: "if you make us look good, you get to stay. If you begin to look better than us, then you've got to go." They would never admit this out loud, but Aaron and his wife were very insecure people and secure people really freaked them out. Here is what Dr. Davis discovered: insecure people do everything in their power to put others down out of jealousy as they lift themselves up. This is what a pandemic of Leader-I-Tis will do to the heart of a leader: it will put good people down and lift up the bad ones. Aaron failed to appreciate and praise others in the organization's successes.

Leadership Failure #6: A Failure To Appreciate And Praise Others In The Organization's Successes

---

Are the leaders willing to share the glory when things are going well?

Are the leaders willing to promote the contributions of those who serve behind the scenes?

"So, Aaron, will you answer my question: why do secure people make you so insecure?" Silence. More silence. Still; even more silence. Dr. Davis had met face to face the infamous blank stare that looked right through you as if you did not exist. Dr. Davis was not the first one to encounter the blank look, but getting the look was everything Dr. Davis needed to know about how to summarize his report.

The "look" is symbolic of what was wrong with this organization. With Aaron's blank stare Dr. Davis rightly concluded that there is no longer any viable life in this organization. Yes, there may be occasional pockets of success in the organization, but because of the infectious spread of Leader-I-Tis even the healthy parts of the organization will eventually become sick and die too.

Interlude:

The story above is a composite and based upon real events that took place over an extended period of time. The names have been changed to protect the guilty. In writing this book I was faced with the unique challenge of not only writing about the leadership disease of Leader-I-Tis but to also offer objective hope to everyone who is "trapped" in a toxic organization. I personally know that the path of working in a toxic organization is difficult and may seem at times to be a doomed life with no relief in sight. But I believe that as long as we have breath, we have hope. We hope that we can live above the fray and, even better, learn how to thrive until we can find a way out.

I make no apologies here. I am a writer who also happens to be a follower of Jesus. I am not simply a Christian writer, but I am a writer who is a Christian. So I am writing from a worldview that may be different from yours. But I invite you to hang around for the next section of the book. What I have already shared with you are leadership principles that are true and are adaptable to all, if not most, organizations—both in non-profit faith-based organizations and in the market place. Section two is my way of integrating the problems of Leader-I-Tis and living above the fray into a Biblical grid where practical answers for the life of a quality leader are spelled out clearly. The best part of this next section is that all of it is TRUE (at least the parts that God gets credit for—His Word!).

If you are suffering from the effects of Leader-I-Tis and are seeking to live above the fray, my prayer for you is that

➢ You will find healing from the One who does the Healing.

➢ You will be clean and useful for the Master to use for His glory.

➢ You will find purpose in what you pursue and you will find the right people to help you in your pursuit of your purpose

➢ You will learn how to effectively relate to difficult people.

➢ You will learn how to watch out for bullies.

➢ You will learn the value of having a mentor in your life (and becoming one too)

➢ You will learn how to apply the Bible to your life.

> ➤ You will learn how to be focused and keep the main thing, the main thing.

Scientists today are still looking for the cure for many horrible diseases. By God's grace, I am privileged to share with you the antidote for the horrible disease called Leader-I-Tis. Lets walk through the healing waters together. The prescription for healthy leadership and living above the fray begins on the next page.

PART TWO:

A BIBLICAL RESPONSE FOR

LIVING ABOVE THE FRAY

[16] Let the message about Christ, in all its richness, fill your lives. Teach and counsel each other with all the wisdom he gives. Sing psalms and hymns and spiritual songs to God with thankful hearts. [17] And whatever you do or say, do it as a representative of the Lord Jesus, giving thanks through him to God the Father. **Colossians 3:16-17 (NLT)**

Seven Biblical Leadership Principles For Living Above The Fray
(2 Timothy 2:20-4:5)

The foundation is the most essential aspect of any building that is to be built. All of the walls, ceilings, and various accessories are useless unless a sure foundation is in place. In order to best understand what it means to live above the fray and how to do it well, a proper understanding from the teaching of Scripture will provide for us the necessary foundation before we move on to anything else. Let's examine seven essential Biblical leadership principles that will enable us to live above the fray.

Leadership Principle One

Stay Useful!

Living Above The Fray Begins Here

We Need To Be Clean And Useful

(2 Timothy 2:20-21)

Everyone thinks of changing the world, but no one thinks of changing himself.

~Leo Nikolaevich Tolstoy

If this principle is not in place, then the other six are

not relevant. There are many who have allowed bitterness and anger to distract them from the goal of being useful to the Lord. There are many who have sipped the Kool-Aid of false teaching and have exchanged the truth that leads to freedom for a lie that binds and imprisons. In other words, it's easy to become dirty, even when "going to church."

[20] Now in a large house there are not only gold and silver vessels, but also vessels of wood and of earthenware, and some to honor and some to dishonor. [21] Therefore, if anyone cleanses himself from these *things,* he will be a vessel for honor, sanctified, useful to the Master, prepared for every good work. **(2 Timothy 2:20-21)**

Note the lessons we can gain from verse 21:

if anyone cleanses himself from these *things:*

There is a condition upon this statement, "if." If anyone "cleanses himself" declares the need to own our stuff and then to make it right. The word "cleanse" literally means to initiate a ritual of cleansing. In a very practical sense it means that one's cleansing must be regular and must be done thoroughly. In order to gain a correct understanding of what Paul is saying to Timothy, we need to unpack the grammar of the word *ekkathare,* "to cleanse."

The mood of the word is *subjunctive,* meaning Paul,

from his perspective is not making an assertion here but is implying a wish or desire about a hypothetical situation. The verb is in the aorist tense, which means the action takes place in the past but may have lasting results in the future. In other words, a decision made in time by Timothy to cleanse himself creates the chance for spiritual momentum to take place in the future as he continues his walk with the Lord. Finally, the grammar indicates the verb "to cleanse" is used in the active voice. This means the "subject", Timothy, is doing the action. No one else is going to cleanse him. No, it will not be Paul; no one in his family. No one can accomplish this task but Timothy.

But to be cleansed from what? In the context of this portion of Scripture, Paul is referring to the toxins of false teachers and their teaching. Here is the greater question that everyone who desires to live above the fray must seriously ask and come to terms with if one wishes to be cleansed: Is it possible for a professing Christian to teach (or even believe) false things? Of course it is. And what kinds of things may contaminate disciples of Jesus?

One example is a twisting of Scripture where a biblical doctrine like submission is wrongly applied. For instance, any kind of constructive feedback or honest questioning of leadership is rejected by leadership. And further more, there are toxic leaders who punish anyone who dares to suggest another perspective. Submission is used like a whip and anyone who refuses to submit will be punished (by God, so they would claim).

Another example of what some need cleansing from false teaching is when toxic church leaders allow the self-promotion of a pastor who becomes greater than the message of the cross. What may have been a humble beginning may over time evolve into a personality cult (or using more biblical terms, it is called idolatry). In some cases, there are some who are expected by the church leadership to turn a blind eye to the personality cult the church leaders are fostering. In some toxic churches, Jesus has been replaced by a leader's charm and manipulation. I'm sure that most leaders do not start this way, but a man can only take so much adoration and worship until he (and his rabid fans) actually believe the messenger becomes more important than the Message.

No doubt, a pastor may faithfully preach the Gospel for many years and experience spiritual fruit. But because of his own shallowness and insecurities he is willing to solicit the praise of others at the expense of enabling a congregation to slip and slide into idolatry . . . of him. His "teaching" from the pulpit may always come from the Bible, but his desire to be a "rock star" will teach other things too.

We rightly think of false teaching as some gross perversion of our sacred doctrines. But the personality worship of charismatic leaders is also another aspect of false teaching. It is not strange to think that since we live in a culture that promotes the adoration of athletes, actors, and musicians, that some of this would seep into the culture of the western church. If you are going to succeed and live above the fray, you've got to stick to His Word and keep Jesus Lord of all.

Perhaps you are swimming in a toxic sea of "these things" and need to be cleansed. Whatever you do, do not swallow the water. Simply get out of the poison and cleanse yourself today. How does one cleanse oneself? The cleaning agent is grace. Wash yourself with it.

"Then I will sprinkle clean water on you, and you will be clean; I will cleanse you from all your filthiness and from all your idols. **Ezekiel 36:25 (NASB95)**

"Every branch in Me that does not bear fruit, He takes away; and every *branch* that bears fruit, He prunes it so that it may bear more fruit. ³ "You are already clean because of the word which I have spoken to you. **John 15:2-3 (NASB95)**

Therefore, having these promises, beloved, let us cleanse ourselves from all defilement of flesh and spirit, perfecting holiness in the fear of God. **2 Corinthians 7:1 (NASB95)**

Draw near to God and He will draw near to you. Cleanse

your hands, you sinners; and purify your hearts, you double-minded. **James 4:8 (NASB95)**

If we confess our sins, He is faithful and righteous to forgive us our sins and to cleanse us from all unrighteousness. **1 John 1:9 (NASB95)**

Here are some final exegetical comments on the remaining devotional points of this verse:

he will be a vessel for honor, sanctified:

This statement means more than having the honor of being used by the Lord. It implies that an inner transformation takes place inside the heart of the believer who chooses to cleanse himself. This "sanctification" means . . .

- The change is taking place from the inside out
- The change is caused by Jesus and His grace
- The change is supernatural, not a natural man-made effort

to the church of God which is at Corinth, to those who have been sanctified in Christ Jesus, saints by calling, with all who in every place call upon the name of our Lord Jesus Christ, their *Lord* and ours: **1 Corinthians 1:2 (NASB77)**

but like the Holy One who called you, be holy yourselves also in all *your* behavior; **1 Peter 1:15 (NASB77)**

For both He who sanctifies and those who are sanctified are all from one *Father*; for which reason He is not ashamed to call them brethren, **Hebrews 2:11 (NASB77)**

But by His doing you are in Christ Jesus, who became to us wisdom from God, and righteousness and sanctification, and redemption, **1 Corinthians 1:30 (NASB77)**

Now may the God of peace Himself sanctify you entirely; and may your spirit and soul and body be preserved complete, without blame at the coming of our Lord Jesus Christ. **1 Thessalonians 5:23 (NASB77)**

useful to the Master:

The word "useful" is pregnant with meaning. It means we have purpose for Kingdom affairs. It means that we are a part of His plan. To be useful means we are part of a cause greater than ourselves. There is no greater joy for the disciple of Jesus not to only realize his or her purpose but to have a useful purpose as well.

And the things which you have heard from me in the presence of many witnesses, these entrust to faithful men, who will be able to teach others also. **2 Timothy 2:2 (NASB77)**

I thank Christ Jesus our Lord, who has strengthened me, because He considered me faithful, putting me into service; **1 Timothy 1:12 (NASB77)**

In this case, moreover, it is required of stewards that one be found trustworthy. **1 Corinthians 4:2 (NASB77)**

[6] For I am already being poured out as a drink offering, and the time of my departure has come. [7] I have fought the good fight, I have finished the course, I have kept the faith; [8] in the future there is laid up for me the crown of righteousness, which the Lord, the righteous Judge, will award to me on that day; and not only to me, but also to all who have loved His

appearing. **2 Timothy 4:6-8 (NASB77)**

prepared for every good work:

When we have made the decision to cleanse ourselves and become a vessel for honor, sanctified and useful to the Master, we will be prepared to do any task the Lord assigns to us, and do it well for His glory.

[8] For by grace you have been saved through faith; and that not of yourselves, *it is* the gift of God; [9] not as a result of works, that no one should boast. [10] For we are His workmanship, created in Christ Jesus for good works, which God prepared beforehand, that we should walk in them. **Ephesians 2:8-10 (NASB77)**

Not to us, O LORD, not to us, But to Thy name give glory Because of Thy lovingkindness, because of Thy truth. **Psalm 115:1 (NASB77)**

Summary:

If you want to live above the fray then . . . **Stay Useful!** You Need To Be Clean And Useful

Reflect and Respond

Apply This Leadership Principle To Your Life

Principle #1: We Need To Be Clean And Useful

(2 Timothy 2:20-21)

1.   Take some time this week and reflect upon any areas in your life that need spiritual cleansing. This is a time of grace, not self-condemnation; a time for cleansing, not for stirring up past failures where you wallow around in the mud.

2.   Consider meditating upon one of the Scriptures mentioned in this chapter. Over the course of a week, read it slowly, contemplate its message, and allow the freeing truth to wash over your heart.

3.   Think about all of the ways that you are "useful" to the Master. Make a bullet list of at least three ways where God has used you for His purpose this week. Be careful not to over spiritualize this exercise. Keep your points practical.

A Prayer Of Application:

Lord Jesus, I desire to live above the fray. I want to be clean and useful. May I take an honest inventory of my heart and see if there is anything in me that is hindering me from being useful to You. Thank You for changing me from the inside out.

Leadership Principle Two

Stay Strategic!

Living Above The Fray Means We Are Intentional In Actions
and In Right Relationships

*Principle #2: We Need To Be Purposeful In What We Pursue And
With Whom We Pursue It*
(2 Timothy 2:22)

*We are known by the company we keep;
and the company we keep will form who we become.*

We live in a culture where the motto has been, "If it feels good, do it." I'm not really sure when I noticed the subtle shift of values in my protected little world called the American dream. I grew up as a child and young person in the 1960's where "free love" was not only preached but was practiced by many. It was the "good ole days" of rock and roll where the name Woodstock would no longer be a farm estate but the term associated with a sexual and drug revolution. For whatever reason, none of that really appealed to me. My parents did a pretty good job of shielding me from experiences that my older friends were diving into. And somehow, by the grace of God, I was blessed to be around other friends who chose not to chase the wrong kind of life. My lusts were more "innocent." (like a rotten thought life that I hid in the depth of my soul).

Now flee from youthful lusts and pursue righteousness, faith, love *and* peace, with those who call on the Lord from a pure heart. **(2 Timothy 2:22)**

In this passage of Scripture, Paul gives a direct command:

Now flee from youthful lusts

This is a powerful phrase given to a believer, a man that Paul had invested in. This admonition was given to Timothy, his spiritual son in the faith. Here is the point: if this was such an intense warning given to a man with a great spiritual foundation, how much more should we heed it too.

The word "flee" means to escape. It means to run away with all abandon, not looking back and certainly not hanging around with the vain idea that we can "negotiate" with these youthful lusts and they will give up and leave us alone. The grammatical construction of this verb is pretty intense. It's not an optional, take it or leave it, command. It is in the "imperative" mode, which simply means, this is a COMMAND! The heart of the word "flee" is also in the "present" tense. It means, do it NOW! We can easily concur that Paul was very serious about youthful lusts. They were a serious challenge to disciples of Jesus in Paul's day and they are just as serious, if not even more so, in our day and time. So, we know we need to flee, but here comes a very logical question: What are "youthful lusts?" Hang around. The answer might be a surprise (and if you are "older" it might even depress you).

A "youthful lust" is nothing more than a simple passion or desire for something. This passion can be just as easily directed to that which is wholesome or that which is evil. The passion we have is not unusual, but quite normal. It is called being human. The problem comes when our cravings, our desires turn into lusts and get out of hand and begin to pull us down into the immoral abyss. Let's illustrate. There is nothing inherently wrong with desiring a good job. The lust comes when we desire the money we make more than we desire to have a relationship with the Lord. Another example: it is completely normal to admire the beauty of another person. But when lust hijacks desire and begins to crave, to lust for someone in an improper fashion, we have crossed over into youthful lusts.

To clarify, we are to flee youthful lusts. So, exactly what are some of these youthful lusts and how can they become a snare trap to us? One example is the desire to be accepted by others. This is okay, but it can easily turn into an obsession to be liked. Another youthful lust is when we no longer become satisfied with what the Lord has provided for us. Because of lust, we crave another illicit relationship, we want more material things, and we are not satisfied or content, but empty and needing more. And here is one youthful lust that many narcissistic leaders must flee, or else: the need to be the center of attention. This is the craving to be the best dressed, most noticed, most heard, and most important person in the room (at least in their mind).

Now, here is the challenge. We hear what Paul is forcefully saying, "Get away, far away, quickly, from youthful lusts." Okay, but how? Do we have to do this heavy-duty spiritual lifting alone, or is help on the way? There are some things we must do besides run away. We are to run towards something too. The answer to our need is given in this next portion of the Scripture:

pursue righteousness, faith, love *and* peace

As we are to flee youthful lusts, so must we not live in a vacuum and do nothing. With just as much force as the word "flee," we are to "pursue." Like the grammar in "flee," this verb, "to pursue" is an imperative command and the tense of the verb is in the present. It means "to strongly follow after, to press on towards, to press forward." We are to *pursue* four spiritual qualities.

We are to pursue *"righteousness."* What does it mean to pursue this quality? It means that we are to pursue a righteousness that is right with God and embrace a life that is lived in a right way.

We are to pursue *"faith."* When fleeing youthful lusts, we are to strongly follow after God and believe Him as well as being faithful to the Lord.

We are to pursue *"love."* When we are pursuing love, it means we are pressing forward towards experiencing agape, the God kind of love. This is the love that is selfless and sacrificial.

We are to pursue *"peace."* When we pursue peace we are racing towards a new way of living that the world does not understand but so desperately needs to experience. This peace means we are resting in the secure arms of our Savior. This peace means that no matter how chaotic our outer world might be, our inner world (our heart and our mind) are covered by His peace.

Finally, note this perspective: we are not called to pick and choose from our four "favorite" qualities. We are to pursue all of them. Righteousness, faith, love, and peace.

Now, the fun really begins. We don't have to live the

Christian life ALONE! We are to flee as fast as we can from the bad stuff and run as hard as we can towards the good stuff with this tribe of people:

with those who call on the Lord from a pure heart.

This phrase reminds us of the kind of spiritual company whom we are to surround ourselves: we are to live the Christian life with those who call on the Lord from a pure heart. Choose the wrong crowd, and the chances are pretty good that we will find ourselves in a lousy set of circumstances. However, choose the right people who will cheer us on, love on us, forgive us, pour out grace upon us, and at times correct us and we will be on the path to spiritual success.

What does it mean to call on the Lord from a pure heart? The Greek word used is *"katharos."* It means "clean, clear, pure." Everyone who has been given a pure heart from the Lord did not work hard enough or be good enough to have one. Like me, and like you, a pure heart comes as a direct result of the work Jesus did for us on the Cross. And like me, and like you, we have the incredible ability to mess up every day. Mercifully, God has made a way for us to have a pure heart every day.

David experienced our dilemma of sin. Listen to how he approached it. He asked God to create (to make something out of nothing—what a miracle!) a clean heart:

Create in me a clean heart, O God, And renew a steadfast spirit within me. **Psalm 51:10 (NASB77)**

The apostle John shares this antidote for the problem of unconfessed sin:

If we confess our sins, He is faithful and righteous to forgive us our sins and to cleanse us from all unrighteousness. **1 John 1:9 (NASB77)**

Summary:

If you want to live above the fray then . . . **Stay Strategic!**
You Need To Be Purposeful In What You Pursue And With Whom You Pursue It

Reflect and Respond

Apply This Principle To Your Life

Principle #2: We Need To Be Purposeful In What We Pursue And With Whom We Pursue It (2 Timothy 2:22)

1.   Take time for some honesty this week. What are some of the "youthful lusts" that intrigue you? Is there any passion that has entangled you that may put you in danger of being burned? If no one knew but you and God, would you give in to get it?

2.   What is your exit strategy when confronted by a youthful lust? Perhaps it would be helpful to you (and even hold yourself accountable) to write down your exact plan for your way of escape.

3.   It is near to impossible to live the victorious Christian life alone. Who are the people in your inner circle who have agreed to pursue an authentic relationship with Jesus? We need to be with the right crowd who loves and cheers each other on. Make a list of those people and then offer a prayer of thanksgiving to God for their heart for the Lord, and for you.

A Prayer Of Application:

Lord Jesus, I desire to live above the fray. I want to be purposeful in what I pursue and with whom I pursue it.

Leadership Principle Three

Stay Alert!

Living Above The Fray Insists We Exhibit
Excellent People Skills

*Principle #3: We Need To Learn How To Effectively
Relate To Difficult People
(2 Timothy 2:23-26)*

*We find comfort among those who agree with us –
growth among those who don't. ~ Frank A. Clark*

*Don't say, "That person bothers me."
Think: "That person sanctifies me."
Josemaria Escriva, founder of Opus Dei*

"Its not fair!" These are the words spoken in many languages around the world everyday—and by now, I'm certain that many of you have come to believe by your own experience that life is not fair. You can do all of the right things in the right way and still be treated unfairly. Ask Joseph, Daniel, and Jesus; just to name a few who were treated unfairly. Feel free to add you name to the list, if you wish. When we are treated unfairly, it is easy to rise up and go into the attack mode. No matter where we work or where we play or even where we go to church, we will have to face difficult people. The key for us is simply this: how can we best relate to them and do what is right (and live above the fray)? Perhaps, this illustration will help bring clarity to you.

"This moment had been brewing for years. The in-my-face lack of professional respect, the personal distain directed toward me (and others), and in spite of my best efforts to peacefully coexist with the organization's leader, the relationship was beyond repair. I was accused during a staff meeting that I was "too nice" by the leader of my organization and needed to, in his words, "toughen up." In other words, I needed to learn how to throw down word bombs too. His volcanic words were insulting, demeaning, and full of poisonous venom. Instead of seeking to create an environment of peace, the DNA of the organizational culture was to keep everyone who refused to "fight" him on eggshells, waiting for the next explosion of his temper to rain down."

No doubt, this leader was the classic "workplace bully." Honestly, for all of us, there would be the temptation to throw back at him harsh and biting words that would even the score and make him feel our pain. Tempting yes, but at what price to us? Jesus has a better idea of a more biblical response when He said to turn the other cheek.

[38] " You have heard that it was said, ' AN EYE FOR AN EYE, AND A TOOTH FOR A TOOTH.' [39] "But I say to you, do not resist him who is evil; but whoever slaps you on your right cheek, turn to him the other also. **Matthew 5:38-**

39 (NASB77)

There are some great lessons for living above the fray from these important portions of Scripture. Lets review them:

[23] But refuse foolish and ignorant speculations, knowing that they produce quarrels. [24] The Lord's bond-servant must not be quarrelsome, but be kind to all, able to teach, patient when wronged, [25] with gentleness correcting those who are in opposition, if perhaps God may grant them repentance leading to the knowledge of the truth, [26] and they may come to their senses *and escape* from the snare of the devil, having been held captive by him to do his will. **(2 Timothy 2:23-26)**

But refuse foolish and ignorant speculations, knowing that they produce quarrels.

It is possible to win the argument but lose the relationship. Even if we have the winning argument and the facts are on our side, there are some occasions where we need to not engage with quarrelsome people. Some people live to argue and are not satisfied until we engage with them and become quarrelsome too. There are some things that we do need to do. We do need to enter the arena of ideas and contribute—to the things that matter. What Paul is referring to here is vain things, useless facts, foolish and ignorant speculations. Words are too precious to waste on people and arguments that have no positive merit. We can do much better than this.

The Lord's bond-servant must not be quarrelsome, but be kind to all, able to teach, patient when wronged, with gentleness correcting those who are in opposition, if perhaps God may grant them repentance leading to the knowledge of the truth,

We have no control over what other people say and do. But disciples who follow Jesus do have control over what they say and do. We are exhorted to live in a dynamic way by living out these five qualities. If we know them and live them well, we will be well on our way to living above the fray.

1.   *We must not be quarrelsome.* This word *machomai,* (its where we get the term "macho man") means to fight, to argue, to quarrel. Yes, there is an inner tension to lash out; especially when we think we are right and we need to prove it to anyone who may doubt that we are right.

2.   *We must be kind to all.* The word kind can also be translated as gentle or mild. The word kind means that we are to be reasonable and considerate. While some will return an insult with an insult, the command of this scripture instructs us to respond in a completely different way.

3.   *We must be able to teach.* By no means does this mean we are to find a classroom and have everyone sit in desks and be lectured by us. What it does mean is this: it means that we are to have an ability to teach, in the moment. We need to be skilled in knowing what to say and how to say it in a way the truth will be received. We will see the significance of this quality later on in this passage of Scripture and the kind of impact we can have on difficult, hard to get along with, people.

4.   *We must be patient when wronged.* Perhaps this may be the greatest challenge in this list of five actions. When we are wronged it is normal to defend and retaliate. But note the meaning of the word "patient." We must "endure evil." The heart of being patient is made possible because of grace. Grace is free. Grace is patient. God is patient too. And He is patient with us. So, because grace is free and because God is patient with us, we are to give both away (grace and patience) to people who do not deserve them. One of the great benefits of being patient with hard to get along with people is it gives God some room to work in their heart.

5.   *We must with gentleness correct those who are in opposition.* Instead of offering quarrelsome people a piece of our mind, we are to take the approach of humility. We are to use gentleness to correct those who oppose us. What kind of

"rule" is this? This makes no sense to the normal mind. But there is a greater purpose here of not losing the relationship in order to win the argument: if we say the right thing and do the right thing, our response allows for this supernatural possibility: "if perhaps God may grant them repentance leading to the knowledge of the truth."

Here is the bottom line to living above the fray and why our choice to do so not only impacts us. To an even greater degree, our decision not to be quarrelsome, to be kind, to teach humbly, to be patient when wronged, and to correct those who oppose us with gentleness, may very well be the catalyst for their spiritual awakening. How we respond, how we live above the fray, may lead to the repentance of the very person who has been getting under our skin.

"and they may come to their senses and escape from the snare of the devil, having been held captive by him to do his will."

Wow! A sound mind as they come to their senses. A person who has escaped, experienced a deliverance from Satan's snare. Spiritual bondage to his will—gone! Isn't this possible outcome an incredible reward for you . . . and for them? When we live above the fray, the possibility for transformed lives exists . . . in us, and in those who oppose us.

Summary:

If you want to live above the fray then . . . **Stay Alert!** You Need To Learn How To Effectively Relate To Difficult People

Reflect and Respond

Apply This Principle To Your Life

Principle #3: We Need To Learn How To Effectively
Relate To Difficult People (2 Timothy 2:23-26)

1.   Spend some time this week and go over in your mind those intense conversations where you felt at a loss for the right words. For example, "I wish I would have said that!" or "I wish I could eat the words that left my mouth too soon." Give yourself permission to go back and rewrite the script. Some of our greatest lessons are learned when we go back and review and rehearse for the next time.

2.   Who is the most difficult person you know? What makes them that way? Spend some time and prayerfully come up with a strategy on the best way you can deal with them.

3.   Grace-filled people tend to be Grace-driven people too. Take some time this week and mediate on how grace can help you deal with hard to get along with people.

A Prayer Of Application:

Lord Jesus, I desire to live above the fray. I want to learn how to effectively relate to difficult people. Your grace is free. Your grace is patient. You are patient too. And You are patient with me. Help me give away grace to those who do not deserve it.

Leadership Principle Four

Stay Strong!

Living Above The Fray Means We Refuse To Sink
To The Level Of Those Who Sin Against Us

Principle #4: We Need To Beware Of The People
Who Are Bullies
(2 Timothy 3:1-9)

In hindsight, I slid into arrogance based upon past success.
Reed Hastings

Pride makes us artificial and humility makes us real.
Thomas Merton

The pen is mightier than the sword.
Edward Bulwer-Lytton

Narcissus was a young man, according to Greek
mythology, who was enamored with his beauty. Staring into
the stream, he leaned over and gazed with a power that would
not allow him to pull back. He became so mesmerized by his
reflected image that he became a prisoner of his own ego. He
fell into the water and drowned. And as the legend has it, he
turned into a flower called the Narcissus, which bloomed at
the edge of the stream.

Narcissus is a myth, but his story represents the kind of people we are to avoid. And may I add, the kind of people we do not want to become! Some call them "center-stage people." Another descriptive word is "self-centered." Some use the term "rock star" to describe the narcissist. In the heart of hearts, the narcissist is convinced that the world revolves around him or her and they see it as their moral obligation to convince everyone around them of that fact.

We are engaged in a great struggle as we live in a culture where we are supposed to get our own way, to do our own thing, and to look out for number one—me. Perhaps without even realizing what is going on, many have enabled the blind ambitions of those who wish to live unaccountable lives. The way of the arrogant, the self-centered, the rebellious, and the abusive is often celebrated (or at least tolerated), not always rejected. When the life of the spiritual narcissist is accepted as the norm, "group think" takes over and then any kind of rebuke is seen as judging or unfairly critical. In this crazy world, political correctness has run amuck, even among people who claim to be a Christian and go to church.

Now here is the danger of which Paul is writing. The negative qualities, which are listed in the following verses, are especially appealing to those who feel they are "entitled" because of their position. Like a moth drawn to the flame, they do not think twice about being lovers of self, lovers of money, boastful, arrogant, revilers, etc. Those who have a serious case of spiritual narcissism are drawn to these attributes. In a moment we are going to take a closer look at each one of these negative characteristics, but before then, allow me to share a story with you that will illustrate one way narcissistic leaders can bring harm to their organization.

I always believed that bullies were confined to two places: on the school playground during recess and on the school bus coming home. I also believed that once young bullies grew up they would outgrow their innate need to keep on bullying others. I was mistaken. Young bullies also grow up and remain bullies. They have had plenty of time to refine their "art" as adults. One would think that bullying only takes place in the school playground or on the job site, but in a church? Really? Yes, really. That's where I met my bullies.

There are some people who use their "power" to manipulate others in order to get their way. Leading out of fear and their own insecurity, the workplace bully seeks to intimidate others to cower and bow down. The great and wonderful Wizard of Oz is a revealing illustration of the classic bully. He was all about himself in the bully mode when the curtain was closed. But it was brave Toto, the wonder dog, who pulled the curtain back revealing a boisterous man who lost all of his courage when he was revealed. The pulling back of the curtain also gave instant courage to those who were being bullied. An important principle to remember is that spiritual bullying can cause great harm and it needs to be exposed. As the spiritual bully surrounds himself with his or her protective entourage, danger looms for the disciple of Jesus. This passage of Scripture reminds us of how serious it is:

And men will rise up from your own number with deviant doctrines to lure the disciples into following them. **Acts 20:30 (HCSB)**

There are many deviant doctrines from which we can pick and choose. In this case, the deviant doctrine I am underscoring is the personality cult, where people with apparent good sense are deluded by the power of the spiritual bully.

Now, lets unpack this list of the qualities of dangerous people.

[1] But realize this, that in the last days difficult times will come. [2] For men will be lovers of self, lovers of money, boastful, arrogant, revilers, disobedient to parents, ungrateful, unholy, [3] unloving, irreconcilable, malicious gossips, without self-control, brutal, haters of good, [4] treacherous, reckless,

conceited, lovers of pleasure rather than lovers of God, [5] holding to a form of godliness, although they have denied its power; Avoid such men as these. [6] For among them are those who enter into households and captivate weak women weighed down with sins, led on by various impulses, [7] always learning and never able to come to the knowledge of the truth. [8] Just as Jannes and Jambres opposed Moses, so these *men* also oppose the truth, men of depraved mind, rejected in regard to the faith. [9] But they will not make further progress; for their folly will be obvious to all, just as Jannes's and Jambres's folly was also. **(2 Timothy 3:1-9)**

[1] But realize this, that in the last days difficult times will come.

It is important to remember that Paul wrote these words to Timothy over 2,000 years ago. I believe that we are in the last days and the difficult times are here. This "prophecy" has come true. Now what? These words are given to us in order that we might be emotionally and spiritually prepared for some very difficult, uneasy, dangerous, and trying times. The people who live ungodly lives will be marked by these eighteen qualities:

[2] For men will be lovers of self, lovers of money, boastful, arrogant, revilers, disobedient to parents, ungrateful, unholy, [3] unloving, irreconcilable, malicious gossips,

without self-control, brutal, haters of good, ⁴ treacherous, reckless, conceited, lovers of pleasure rather than lovers of God, ⁵ holding to a form of godliness, although they have denied its power; Avoid such men as these.

(1) What does it mean to be a "lover of self?" It means to be self-centered or narcissistic. It is the ultimate form of idolatry—the worship of one's own self. (1 John 3:17)

(2) What does it mean to be a "lover of money?" It means to covet and be consumed by materialism. The person who is a lover of money is also a hoarder of money too. (1 Tim. 6:10)

(3) What does it mean to be "boastful?" It means to be braggadocios, to make an open show to impress others. This person is the one who talks big but rarely has anything to show for it. (Prov. 25:14)

(4) What does it mean to be "arrogant?" It means to be full of pride, to be conceited, to be haughty. This is the person who sees himself as better than anyone else. The arrogant person uses other people to get what he wants. (Matt. 23:12)

(5) What does it mean to be a "reviler?" It means to be abusive of others. It means to slander or insult. The NLT translates the word as "scoffing at God." The word comes from the root word, "blaspheme." It is true that men do blaspheme God in a direct way, but men can also blaspheme

God in an indirect way when people who are made in His own image are insulted. (James 3:8-9)

(6) What does it mean to be "disobedient to parents?" It means to show a lack of respect, to dishonor, to rebel against. If rebellion thrives in the home then no society is safe from its toxic poison. (Eph. 6:1-3)

(7) What does it mean to be "ungrateful?" It means to take for granted, to be unthankful, a gross lack of appreciation. The ungrateful person thinks he is "entitled" to what he has been given. (1 Thess. 5:18)

(8) What does it mean to be "unholy?" It means to be shameless, to consider nothing sacred. This person is given over to an unfettered lifestyle, disavowing any sense of decency. (2 Peter 3:11)

(9) What does it mean to be "unloving?" It means to be without love or heartless. This person is stoic and without human emotion. The unloving person displays no affection or empathy at all. (Rom. 12:9-10)

(10) What does it mean to be "irreconcilable?" It means to be untrustworthy, to betray, to be a covenant breaker, to be unforgiving. This is the person who makes a commitment but breaks his word. (Eph. 4:25)

(11) What does it mean to be a "malicious gossip?" It means

to slander. The root of this word is where we get our word "devil." The malicious gossip is the person who uses words to destroy with his tongue. (James 3:3-12)

(12) What does it mean to be "without self-control?" It means to lack focus, to be undisciplined, to be powerless, impotent. The person without self-control is out of control. They become slaves to their bad habits and leave a trail of destruction in their path. (Rom. 6:12)

(13) What does it mean to be "brutal?" It means to be savage, untamed or cruel. This is the person who has no conscience and derives a sick pleasure in hurting other people, deeply. (Eph. 4:32)

(14) What does it mean to be a "hater of good?" It means to despise what is good as well as those who are good. This person who is a hater of good despises people who embody "goodness." The spirit of haters of good is so intense it can even intimidate other people into joining them in their hatred of good people. (Titus 1:8)

(15) What does it mean to be "treacherous?" It means to betray, to not protect. This is the person who leaves a trusting person unprotected and betrays them. (James 4:17)

(16) What does it mean to be "reckless?" It means to act rashly, to make a hasty decision without regard to any future

consequences. The reckless person thinks only of himself. Great harm often comes to the organization a reckless person leads. (Prov. 21:5)

(17) What does it mean to be "conceited?" It means to be puffed up with pride. This is the person who has a higher view of himself due to previous achievement. Some handle success well and do so with humility. The conceited person is destroyed by success. (Gal. 6:3)

(18) What does it mean to be a "lover of pleasure rather than a lover of God?" It means to place more value on the temporal than the eternal. It means that we idolize what brings us pleasure instead of loving and worshiping God. (Matt. 6:33)

All of these eighteen characteristics lead to this powerful summation:

[This kind of person is] holding to a form of godliness, although they have denied its power; Avoid such men as these.

Or more clearly stated by the New Living Translation,

They will act religious, but they will reject the power that could make them godly. Stay away from people like that! **2 Timothy 3:5 (NLT)**

What does it mean to hold to a form of godliness? It means to have an outward, visible form. It means that this kind of person will act religious. They know the "Christian language" by heart. They know how to act and what to say. They frequent Christian gatherings as a religious duty, rarely missing a scheduled event. And yet, THEY REJECT THE POWER THAT COULD MAKE THEM GODLY. This leads me to offer a series of key questions: What if Paul is talking about people who profess Jesus as their Savior? What if Paul has made this lengthy list of eighteen characteristics of people to warn us about those who have rejected the grace-driven life for the works-driven life? What if some professing Christians start running the race well, but get off course and fall into deception?

Listen carefully to what I say. The only power that is going to change us is the power of the Gospel. Now listen even closer: The Gospel of Jesus (The Good News) not only is given to save us but the Gospel (The Good News) also gives us the power to live the Christian life as Jesus designed us to live. If what I say is true, then what is to be our response to these kinds of people? Paul commands us to "Stay away from people like that!" Stay away from those who may talk the talk but have no intention to walking the walk.

But what do you do when you've done all you know

to do to avoid and stay away from these kinds of people, but still find yourself having to deal with them? What then? In my research I've come across many challenging stories similar to mine. Here is one account, of many, that might even resonate with your experience.

"It seemed the harder I tried to be at peace with the leader of my organization, the more challenging it became. He was a confrontation waiting to happen. When a conversation among staff was becoming intense, instead of adding more fuel to the fire, I chose not to allow the meeting to escalate. And in so doing, it bought me some time before the next confrontation. I've learned along the way that sometimes, no matter how hard you try to avoid a confrontational person, they will come and find you. He found me a month or so later. This time, the attacks upon me became even more personal. Looking around the room for some kind of help, I found none to be had. Those who did have the power to protect chose to protect themselves instead and allowed me to experience the verbal slaughter."

Here is what I learned about living above the fray. There are no guarantees we will not go through times of intense suffering at the hands of those who have all of the power in the room. Your situation may be awkward and deeply troubling on so many levels. You may love where you work but the work environment has become toxic. There may be many good people in place but they fail to lead and protect you on their watch. You face a serious choice of the heart: will you continue to be the victim or will you become the victor instead? For us, the challenge is will we allow our negative experiences to embitter us or will we rise to the occasion and walk in forgiveness?

Years ago, this is what I did. I prayed. For a month I prayed these words for the man who so hurt and offended me, "God have mercy on *him*." I prayed this prayer every day for two weeks. At the end of the second week, I added this prayer for the other leaders who failed me to my daily office (prayer cycle): "God have mercy on *him* and God have mercy on *them*." I prayed this prayer for a week. Then, in the fourth week I added this prayer for him and them with this: "God have mercy on *him* and God have mercy on *them* and God have mercy on *me*."

By the end of the week of praying that prayer, the Lord answered my prayer (and least I know He did for *me*). I believe that in God's mercy He released me and in so doing freed me from a place of spiritual bullying and emotional abuse to a place of eventual restoration and renewal. If you want to live above the fray, you've got to love the hard to love people and you've got to pray for those who have hurt you and disappointed you. And just as important, you've got to pray for yourself too.

Finally, Paul closes out his thoughts with this illustration.

⁶ For among them are those who enter into households and captivate weak women weighed down with sins, led on by various impulses, ⁷ always learning and never able to come to the knowledge of the truth. ⁸ Just as Jannes and Jambres opposed Moses, so these *men* also oppose the truth, men of depraved mind, rejected in regard to the faith. ⁹ But they will not make further progress; for their folly will be obvious to all, just as Jannes's and Jambres's folly was also.

There are some people who will never "get it." People who allow themselves to be under the influence of spiritual bullies or false teachers, will be always learning and never be able to come to the knowledge of the truth. There will always be people who reject the truth. Don't become one of them. When is the best time to transition? The best time to leave an unhealthy toxic spiritual relationship is now.

Summary:

If you want to live above the fray then . . . **Stay Strong!** You Need To Beware Of The People Who Are Bullies

Reflect and Respond

Apply This Principle To Your Life

*Principle #4: We Need To Beware Of The People
Who Are Bullies (2 Timothy 3:1-9)*

1.   Spend some time this week pondering this statement:
"When I have power do I abuse it or use it to help others?"
Power or authority is a stewardship issue. Use it wisely and
the people are blessed. Abuse it? Well, you know where that
leads.

2.   What kinds of safeguards have I integrated into my
life that will keep me from manifesting those eighteen
ungodly qualities? How do I protect myself from the wrath of
those who exhibit those qualities?

3.   Prayer is an important ingredient when dealing with
toxic leaders who are abusing others. Prayer is a wonderful
bridge between where you are and where the Lord is leading
you. In what way are you praying for them . . . and for you?

A Prayer Of Application:

*Lord Jesus, I desire to live above the fray. I want to beware of the people
who abuse other people through spiritual bullying. I refuse to sink to the
level of those who sin against me.*

Leadership Principle Five

Stay Connected!

Living Above The Fray Requires Good Mentors

Principle #5: We Need To Seek Out The Kinds Of Leaders Who Live Out What They Teach And Believe And Follow Their Example (2 Timothy 3:10-15)

People may not remember exactly what you did or what you said, but they will always remember how you made them feel.

"Those who loved you and were helped by you will remember you. So carve your name on hearts and not on marble." ~ C. H. Spurgeon

It has been said, "Experience is the best guide in life." The truth is *guided experience* is the best guide! Time, money, and emotional energy can be saved by linking up with a person who already understands where you are, where you want to go, and has a good grasp on how to lead you there in a positive way. Everyone needs to have a good mentor. I've been blessed to have four of them. Two of them imparted their guided experience to me in my early twenties. One of them invested in me within the past five years, and the most recent one, became my coach less than a year ago. Allow me to introduce each one of them to you. In fairness, each of my mentors would require an entire book of their own in order for you to understand the full measure of impact they have had upon my life. I'll try to keep it brief for this introduction.

I have been blessed to have a special relationship with several godly men—all of them have made a tremendous impact upon my spiritual life. I think about a veterinarian from Florence South Carolina who believed in me and, during my college age years, offered me a forum for ministry as his lay-renewal youth leader. Dr. Morris Anderson was not only a mentor, advisor, and friend for me; he also acted like a surrogate father to me. Whenever I came to a life-changing fork-in-the-road decision, it seemed that Morris was always there to hear my heart, to give me godly counsel, and then to support me in whatever I chose to do. Morris was the man who not only believed in me but also allowed me to practice in a real-time ministry setting what I was learning. I'll never forget his challenge to me early on when I wanted to give up and quit: *"There are two kinds of people: those who marvel and those who are marveled at. Which one do you want to become?"*

Knox Sherer is the perfect example of a man who sacrificially poured his life into young people. It wasn't like he had nothing else to do. He was a vice-president of his company that kept him extremely busy. He was also married and had two children to raise. In his "other job" Knox was the leader of a ministry called Reach Out, Inc. This ministry was founded in 1973 in order to provide opportunities to introduce young people to the Gospel, mentor them, and empower them to serve. Knox (affectingly known as "Poppa Knox") had no problem delegating responsibilities to young people. He was the overseer of the ministry, but young people and others like me ran the place.

The hub of the ministry was a hangout called "The Door." It was a coffee house that hosted weekly Bible studies and weekend concerts, drawing in musical artists who were on the cutting edge of the music of the Jesus movement. From the coffee house came our own musical groups. I was a member of one, The Reach Out Singers. It was here where I learned how much power music had upon an audience and upon those who performed it. I also learned a lot about worship and humility. Knox never let us forget *Who* we were representing.

I will always be indebted to my friend and mentor, Dr. Rick Higgins. I first met Rick in 2006 upon my return visit to Columbia International University (CIU). I had already graduated there in 1985 with a Masters in Divinity (MDiv) and was now enrolled in the doctoral program. His class on spiritual formation and mentoring impacted me on many levels. It was his course that "validated" what I believe

God has called me to do: *My life mission is to live as a disciple of Jesus Christ and inspire others to do the same.* Rick not only talked and taught about this subject, he was living it out in a way that was so authentic to me. On top of all that, for some reason, a bond of friendship was formed between us.

He became the safe place to share my burdens of the ministry. He became my advisor. He became the chairman of my dissertation committee. He became the consistent cheerleader for me during the endless rewrites of my proposal. Most of all, he became my friend. This is one of the unique blessings of mentoring another person. Without a relationship, mentoring becomes simply a programmatic, hollow approach to life.

My last mentor I met while in my doctoral program. The first time I laid eyes on him, something inside of me said, "you've got to find a way to connect with that guy." Dr. Al McKechnie is the founding director of the pastoral counseling program at CIU. Before he came to CIU, he served as the director of counseling at Bill Hyble's Willow Creek Church. In the early stages of my program I was able to take a couple of his classes, but I wanted more. That would have to wait . . . until the Spring of 2012. I was experiencing extreme pressures in my life. My role as a staff pastor was crushing the life out of me. I needed a coach, a *life* coach. Al joined my team and walked with me for a remarkable ten months. On our journey together, he had a front row seat in my life's unfolding story. He walked me through the waters of employment termination, the feelings of anger and rejection, the unknown journey forward in starting a brand new career and ministry, the constant swings of emotion, and the hopes and dreams that died as quickly as they rose.

At the beginning of our journey together, with checkbook in hand, I inquired from Al what fee he charged for his coaching services. His response surprised me: "I barter in chocolates." I suppose each man has his price, doesn't he? A large reason why this book is now a reality is because of my friend Al. He encouraged me to write it, listened carefully to the process, and was my voice of reason. Vicariously, Al lived most of it with me, and I'm glad he did. If you are wondering if you can buy a copy of this book for a box of chocolates, lets talk about it. My preference is dark chocolate mint.

Those are four mini-stories of four mentors who helped form me into the man I am today. If you don't have one, get one. In fact, get more than one. Diversity is a great thing when it comes to mentoring. No one has all of the experiences and all of the answers. And consider this invitation as well: if you are a disciple of Jesus, whom are you mentoring? God desires that all of us become a disciple maker for Jesus. Now, lets take a look at the text below and learn from Paul what it means to be a mentor and what it means to follow one.

[10] Now you followed my teaching, conduct, purpose, faith, patience, love, perseverance, [11] persecutions, *and* sufferings, such as happened to me at Antioch, at Iconium *and* at Lystra; what persecutions I endured, and out of them all the Lord rescued me! [12] Indeed, all who desire to live godly in Christ Jesus will be persecuted. [13] But evil men and impostors will proceed *from bad* to worse, deceiving and being deceived. [14] You, however, continue in the things you have learned and become convinced of, knowing from whom you have learned *them,* [15] and that from childhood you have known the sacred writings which are able to give you the wisdom that leads to salvation through faith which is in Christ Jesus. **(2 Timothy 3:10-15)**

There is a weighty responsibility when it comes to leadership. What we model (how we live and what we say) is noticed and often imitated. If we model with clarity and do it with excellence, we have the honor of helping others find their way. Note what Paul was requesting of Timothy to imitate and eventually reproduce in others (2 Tim. 2:2).

[10] Now you followed my teaching, conduct, purpose,

faith, patience, love, perseverance, [11] persecutions, *and* sufferings, such as happened to me at Antioch, at Iconium *and* at Lystra; what persecutions I endured, and out of them all the Lord rescued me!

What does it mean to "follow?" It means not to only follow closely, but to investigate it too. Paul's use of the Greek word *parekolouthesas* is significant. He is making an assertion, a strong desire or command to follow. Paul leaves nothing to chance with what he means: "Do it! And as you do follow closely there may be lasting results in the future as well." Paul's charge to Timothy was to follow eight characteristics/practices (or spiritual disciplines) of living the Christian life.

1. What did he mean when he said to *"follow my teaching?"* He meant that Timothy should follow closely Paul's instructions, his "doctrine," his system of belief. It is important to note that Paul's teaching was not based upon popular opinion nor was his teaching rooted in the ways of the world. Paul's source material was the Word of God: the Old Testament Scriptures and the Incarnate Word of God, Jesus. A good mentor knows what he or she believes and is able to clearly explain the truth to the mentoree.

2. What did he mean when he said to *"follow my conduct?"* A good mentor not only talks a good talk, he or she also walks a

good walk too. In order to teach the Christian life, one must also have the credibility to live out what he or she believes. There must be no confusion between what is said and what is done.

3. What did he mean when he said to *"follow my purpose?"* What is one's purpose? The desire to know one's purpose has made Rick Warren's best selling book, "The Purpose-Driven Life" one of the most read books of all time. Why? Because people have this inner craving to do something and believe something that really matters in the big picture of life. A purpose is one's destiny, one's reason for living, one's focused goal for life. In Paul's case, his purpose or aim was to share the Gospel with everyone he came into contact. He was never diverted off message into the trivial topics that distract so many. When we are following the right purpose, we are keeping the main thing, the main thing: Jesus is Lord.

4. What did he mean when he said to *"follow my faith?"* It is interesting how Paul invited Timothy to closely follow his faith. On the surface, this can come across as exclusive, narrow minded or in the vernacular of today's culture, rather intolerant. Faith, the right faith, is an important component in the life of the disciple of Jesus. A faith built on presumption will *disappoint*. A faith that is built upon wrong belief will *deceive*. But a faith built upon the truth of Jesus will *deliver*.

5. What did he mean when he said to *"follow my patience?"* For many of us, this does not seem to be very appealing. Yes, we would love to draw near and closely follow those things that are easy to do. But patience? What is Paul saying? He is saying we need to endure and press on, even when things are not going our way. We need to persevere and trust the process we are in instead of bailing out too quickly and missing the blessing of patience.

6. What did he mean when he said to *"follow my love?"* On the surface, this does not seem to be very demanding or complicated. But what does it mean to closely follow the love of a man like Paul? Love, this kind of love, goes where many fear to go. This kind of love chooses to love the unlovely. It embraces one's enemies and does not hold back. This is the kind of love that has no strings attached. It has been freely received (When Jesus gave it to Paul) and it is freely given away. In another portion of Scripture, Paul charges other believers not to become stagnant in their love but to keep it growing.

[9] But we don't need to write to you about the importance of loving each other, for God himself has taught you to love one another. [10] Indeed, you already show your love for all the believers throughout Macedonia. Even so, dear brothers and sisters, we urge you to love them even more. **1 Thessalonians 4:9-10 (NLT)**

7. What did he mean when he said to *"follow my perseverance?"*

The word he chose means to be steadfast, enduring, to have an inner fortitude. The grammar of the word indicates an active posture, not a passive one. Following the line of reasoning of the need for assertion, it is impossible to hold your ground if you are taking measured steps of retreat. Context is everything when seeking to discover the meaning of Scripture. It's important to observe Paul's life up to this point, as he writes his final book, his last will and testament if you will, to Timothy. Here is a portion of his life journey as a follower of Jesus. When he tells Timothy (and us) to follow closely his perseverance, this is why he gains incredible credibility to speak on the subject:

[23] Are they servants of Christ? I know I sound like a madman, but I have served him far more! I have worked harder, been put in prison more often, been whipped times without number, and faced death again and again. [24] Five different times the Jewish leaders gave me thirty-nine lashes. [25] Three times I was beaten with rods. Once I was stoned. Three times I was shipwrecked. Once I spent a whole night and a day adrift at sea. [26] I have traveled on many long journeys. I have faced danger from rivers and from robbers. I have faced danger from my own people, the Jews, as well as from the Gentiles. I have faced danger in the cities, in the deserts, and on the seas. And I have faced danger from men who claim to be believers but are not. [27] I have worked hard and long, enduring many sleepless nights. I have been hungry and thirsty and have often gone without food. I have shivered in the cold, without enough clothing to keep me warm. [28] Then, besides all this, I have the daily burden of my concern for all the churches. [29] Who is weak without my feeling that

weakness? Who is led astray, and I do not burn with anger? **2 Corinthians 11:23-29 (NLT)**

8. What did he mean when he said to *"follow my persecutions and sufferings?"* See the note above. There is nothing easy about what Paul is commanding the disciple of Jesus to do: to willingly embrace the choice of seeking to know Jesus Christ in a more intimate way. Paul speaks of this clearly when he wrote of his dreams and desires to the Philippians:

I want to know Christ and experience the mighty power that raised him from the dead. I want to suffer with him, sharing in his death, **Philippians 3:10 (NLT)**

In a morbid kind of way, Paul shares with us his "secret sauce" as he lays everything on the line. Dead men have no rights. Dead men no longer have their way. Dead men leave the outcome to the Lord, the Resurrected Lord Jesus. Note the outcome. From Paul's own testimony of following Jesus he was able to emphatically declare: **what persecutions I endured, and out of them all the Lord rescued me!**

Can it be possible that because of Paul's commitment to live out these eight spiritual disciplines that he could be empowered through grace to endure all of his persecutions and sufferings? I think so. And note, he is careful to give praise to the One who made it all possible: The Lord!

And just when you thought it was safe to go outside again, Paul adds one more sobering truth: those who are serious about their walk with Jesus will be (not maybe or might be, but will be) persecuted. And those who oppose the Gospel will become an even greater force for evil against Jesus followers, going from bad to worse.

¹² Indeed, all who desire to live godly in Christ Jesus will be persecuted. ¹³ But evil men and impostors will proceed *from bad* to worse, deceiving and being deceived.

So, what is the strategy now? What are we to do? We need to look to our mentors in the faith. We need to lean toward the godly men and women who not only tell us what to do but to show us how to do it too.

¹⁴ You, however, continue in the things you have learned and become convinced of, knowing from whom you have learned *them,* ¹⁵ and that from childhood you have known the sacred writings which are able to give you the wisdom that leads to salvation through faith which is in Christ Jesus.

Allow me to offer you several closing challenges at the end of this important chapter. First, who are your mentors? Who are the spiritual leaders who will give you guided experience as you live out your faith? Second, whom are you mentoring? Every Paul (or Paulette) needs a Timothy (or Timothea) and every mentoree needs to be helping someone else grow in his or her faith too. In fact, even Paul needed a mentor, someone who could encourage him on his journey. For Paul, it was Barnabus (the son of Encouragement). If you are going to live above the fray, you are going to need some good help along the way. A mentor is exactly what you need.

Summary:

If you want to live above the fray then . . . **Stay Connected!** You Need To Seek Out The Kinds Of Leaders Who Live Out What They Teach And Believe And Follow Their Example

Reflect and Respond

Apply This Principle To Your Life

Principle #5: We Need To Seek Out The Kinds Of Leaders Who Live Out What They Teach And Believe And Follow Their Example (2 Timothy 3:10-15)

1.   Everyone needs someone to show them the ropes; to help them learn how life works. Take some time this week and list at least three individuals who had a tremendous impact upon your life. After making the list, note beside each name why they were such a good mentor for you.

2.   What are some of the attributes you have that attract others to follow you? List several attributes under these three headings: (a) my personality—what is it about my personality that some follow me? (b) my experience—what have I experienced over the years that makes me an attractive mentor? (3) my skill—what am I good at doing that makes people draw closer to me?

3.   Make a list of the people you would love to mentor.

A Prayer Of Application:

Lord Jesus, I desire to live above the fray. I want to seek out the kind of leader who lives out what they teach and believe. I want to follow their example. And may You empower me to be a good mentor too.

Leadership Principle Six

Stay Grounded!

Living Above The Fray Is Fueled By The Study Of And
The Personal Application Of The Bible

Principle #6: We Need To Embrace The Word Of God As Our
Guide So We May Faithfully Live Out The Christian Life
(2 Timothy 3:16-17)

"We can say with confidence that we have never known a man whose life
has changed in any significant way apart from the
regular study of God's Word"
Pat Morley

"Our relationship to the Bible is transformed into a relationship with
the God who speaks to us in and through the Bible"
Scott McKnight

We live in a time in history that Johannes Gutenberg
could never have ever imagined. You may recall that it was
Gutenberg who invented the printing press that had
removable metal dies. On his first run in 1452 he printed 200
Bibles. The world has never been the same since. Now there
are Bibles printed in many different languages. There are also
Bibles that are offered in a plethora of different translations.
In addition, there is no lack for a study Bible, in any

translation, for whatever your interest may be.

You can buy a Bible from the local Christian bookstore or a big box discounter. You can download it, hear it on a podcast, and in some cases even listen to it with beautiful sound effects and realistic background sounds. iPad, iPod, will connect you to the Word of God. Online, offline, the Scriptures are readily available to millions and millions of people around the world. It is one thing to have access to a Bible. It is a far greater thing to read it. It is a much better choice to apply what you are reading.

Here are some questions I would like to pose to you. There are no wrong or right answers; just some good questions for you to ponder. Do you read the Bible for devotion or for study? Do you study God's Word in order to receive guidance or to receive comfort? Do you read through different books of the Bible, one at a time, or do you enjoy doing topical studies instead? Here is the point behind these questions. No matter what hermeneutical approach you take (your method for studying the Bible), you need to be able to read and study God's Word through this prism:

⇒ *Observation*/What is the author of the Bible saying?

⇒ *Interpretation*/What does it mean?

⇒ *Application*/What does it mean to me?

⇒ *Proclamation*/What does it mean through me?

If you take this simple, but efficient approach, you will seldom misuse and wrongly apply (and misunderstand) God's Word. Why is this so important, to get it right when it comes to studying our Bible? Because of the great influence it has upon us as we live out what we believe. Here is the point: If you are going to live above the fray, you are going to have to be grounded in the Word of God.

[16] All Scripture is inspired by God and profitable for teaching, for reproof, for correction, for training in righteousness; [17] so that the man of God may be adequate, equipped for every good work. **(2 Timothy 3:16-17)**

Look closely to how much the Scriptures are essential to the disciple of Jesus Christ.

- It is inspired (all of it) by God
- It is profitable for an abundance of purposes
- It equips us to do everything that God places before us in an excellent way

Systematic study, expository study, devotional study, thematic study should be a part of every believer's Christian experience. If a believer is committed to reading and studying his or her Bible every day, spiritual growth will come. But it is important to note: the goal of Bible study is not just about collecting "Bible trivia." Bible study or Bible "reading" must lead to change, not just for you to be adorned with more intellectual information. In addition, it is imperative that the disciple correctly handles, or "to cut straight" the word of truth (2 Timothy 2:15).

It is essential to understand why a proper understanding and practical application of grace and worship is critical when it comes to the core value of Bible study. Without grace and worship, Bible study becomes nothing more than a religious duty rather than a relational joy. In his book, *The Blue Parakeet: Rethinking How You Read The Bible*, Scot McKnight undergirds this need for a relationship when he writes, "If we are invited to love God by reading the Bible as God's communication with us, then a relational approach to the Bible invites us *to listen to God (the person) speak in the Bible and engage God as we listen* (page 89). . . . A relational approach believes *our relationship to the Bible is transformed into a relationship with the God who speaks to us in and through the Bible*" (page 90).

What are the benefits of being a passionate and careful student of God's Word? It is from the study of God's Word that the disciple gains the assurance of eternal life and answered prayer (1 Jn. 5:13-15). It is from the study of God's Word that the disciple finds instruction concerning endurance, encouragement, and hope (Rom. 15:4). It is from the study of God's Word that the disciple is challenged not only to read the Bible but to hear it and take it to heart (Rev. 1:3).

It is from the study of God's Word that the disciple is encouraged and promised an inheritance (Acts 20:32). It is from the study of God's Word that the disciple is taught, rebuked, corrected, and trained in righteousness (2 Tim. 3:16). "We can say with confidence that we have never known a man whose life has changed in any significant way apart from the regular study of God's Word" (Morley, Delk, & Clemmer: *No man left behind: how to build a thriving disciple-making ministry for every man in your church*. 2006, page 166). It is from the study of God's Word that the disciple is able to discern what other people say is either true or false (Acts 17:11).

It is from the study of God's Word that the disciple learns how to correctly handle the word of truth (2 Tim. 2:15). It is from the study of God's Word that the disciple can prove that Jesus is the Christ, the risen Savior, the Son of God (Jn. 20:31; Acts 18:28). God has given us "wonderful words, marvelous words, wonderful words of life." There is a direct correlation between a commitment to study God's Word and spiritual growth. Brad Waggoner has it right when he writes, "Genuine spiritual formation cannot and will not take place without significant and consistent participation in God's Word" (Waggoner 2008, *The shape of faith to come: spiritual formation and the future of discipleship.* page 76).

Spiritual growth does not come naturally to the believer. It takes an effort on our part in order to grow. Note that salvation is all about Him. We can't do anything to "get" saved. We can't add to it and we sure can't take away from it. Salvation is in and through and by the finished work of Jesus Christ alone. However, God does give us specific tools of grace that we can use in order to enhance our spiritual life. One of the ways in which we can grow is through Bible study. Every believer needs to spend quality time in God's Word.

WHY Are We To Study Our Bible? WHAT Are The Benefits Of Being A Passionate And Careful Student Of God's Word?

1.   It is from the study of God's Word that we gain the assurance of eternal life and answered prayer.

13I write these things to you who believe in the name of the Son of God so that you may know that you have eternal life. 14This is the confidence we have in approaching God: that if we ask anything according to his will, he hears us. 15And if we know that he hears us--whatever we ask--we know that we have what we asked of him. **1 John 5:13-15**

2.   It is from the study of God's Word that we find instruction concerning endurance, encouragement, and hope.

For everything that was written in the past was written to teach us, so that through endurance and the encouragement of the Scriptures we might have hope. **Romans 15:4**

3.   It is from the study of God's Word that we are challenged not to only read the Bible but to hear it and take it to heart.

Blessed is the one who reads the words of this prophecy, and blessed are those who hear it and take to heart what is written in it, because the time is near. **Rev. 1:3**

4.   It is from the study of God's Word that we are encouraged and promised an inheritance.

"Now I commit you to God and to the word of his grace, which can build you up and give you an inheritance among all those who are sanctified. **Acts 20:32**

5.   It is from the study of God's Word that we are taught, rebuked, corrected, and trained in righteousness.

All Scripture is God-breathed and is useful for teaching, rebuking, correcting and training in righteousness, **2 Tim. 3:16**

6.   It is from the study of God's Word that we are able to discern what other people say is either true or false.

Now the Bereans were of more noble character than the Thessalonians, for they received the message with great eagerness and examined the Scriptures every day to see if what Paul said was true. **Acts 17:11**

7.   It is from the study of God's Word that we learn how to correctly handle the word of truth.

Do your best to present yourself to God as one approved, a workman who does not need to be ashamed and who correctly handles the word of truth. **2 Tim. 2:15**

8.   It is from the study of God's Word that we can prove that Jesus is the Christ, the risen Savior, the Son of God.

For he vigorously refuted the Jews in public debate, proving from the Scriptures that Jesus was the Christ. **Acts 18:28**

But these are written that you may believe that Jesus is the Christ, the Son of God, and that by believing you may have life in his name. **John 20:31**

2As his custom was, Paul went into the synagogue, and on three Sabbath days he reasoned with them from the Scriptures, 3explaining and proving that the Christ had to suffer and rise from the dead. "This Jesus I am proclaiming to you is the Christ," he said. **Acts 17:2-3**

God has given us "wonderful words, marvelous words, wonderful words of life." There is a direct correlation between a commitment to study God's Word and spiritual growth. We will never know what God is like until we find out from Him. We will never understand our desperate need for a Savior until we discover how lost we are without Christ. And we will never comprehend how to become more like Jesus until we commit ourselves to becoming a student of the Bible.

Here are some good questions to ponder: How often do you study your Bible? Several times a day? At least once a day? Several times a week? Once a week? Several times a month? Rarely? What steps do you need to take in order to develop a habit of Bible study? How has reading from God's Word benefited you?

It is most likely that the person you disciple will have no greater love and commitment to becoming a student of God's Word than you have. The kind of passion [or lack of passion] you have for the Bible will go a long way in either grounding a person into the truth and becoming a quality disciple or sinking a person into the depths of falsehood and insignificance. Bible study is contagious—pass it on!

HOW Is A Believer To Approach The Scriptures And Study Them? Is There A Right Way To Study God's Word?

1.   In order to correctly study the Bible we need the help of the Holy Spirit.

But the Counselor, the Holy Spirit, whom the Father will send in my name, will teach you all things and will remind you of everything I have said to you. **John 14:26**

2.   In order to correctly study the Bible we need to compare Scripture with Scripture; not a mix of human wisdom with Scripture.

This is what we speak, not in words taught us by human wisdom but in words taught by the Spirit, expressing spiritual truths in spiritual words. **1 Cor. 2:13**

3.   In order to correctly study the Bible we need the help of other teachers when we are uncertain of the meaning of a passage of Scripture.

30Then Philip ran up to the chariot and heard the man reading Isaiah the prophet. "Do you understand what you are reading?" Philip asked.

31"How can I," he said, "unless someone explains it to me?" So he invited Philip to come up and sit with him.

32The eunuch was reading this passage of Scripture:

"He was led like a sheep to the slaughter,

and as a lamb before the shearer is silent,

so he did not open his mouth.

33In his humiliation he was deprived of justice.

Who can speak of his descendants?

For his life was taken from the earth."

34The eunuch asked Philip, "Tell me, please, who is the prophet talking about, himself or someone else?" 35Then Philip began with that very passage of Scripture and told him the good news about Jesus.

36As they traveled along the road, they came to some water and the eunuch said, "Look, here is water. Why shouldn't I be baptized?" 37 38And he gave orders to stop the chariot. Then both Philip and the eunuch went down into the water and Philip baptized him. **Acts 8:30-38**

4.   In order to correctly study the Bible we need be a diligent workman in the Scriptures, not being slack or ashamed.

Do your best to present yourself to God as one approved, a workman who does not need to be ashamed and who correctly handles the word of truth. **2 Tim. 2:15**

5.   *In order to correctly study the Bible we need to study the Scriptures everyday.*

Now the Bereans were of more noble character than the Thessalonians, for they received the message with great eagerness and <u>examined the Scriptures every day</u> to see if what Paul said was true. **Acts 17:11**

Like any good thing in life, there is a right way and a wrong way to do things. The same principle is true about Bible study. It is easy to jump on the bandwagon of the latest spiritual fad at the expense of solid Bible exegesis [study]. There are many sincere people who are coming up with a lot of wrong conclusions about what God has said from His Word. Each disciple has a strong responsibility to study the Bible correctly. A lover of God's Word is a person who is grounded in the Word. And a person who is grounded in the Word will be able to live above the fray.

Summary:

If you want to live above the fray then . . . **Stay Grounded!** You Need To Embrace The Word Of God As Your Guide So You May Faithfully Live Out The Christian Life

Reflect and Respond

Apply This Principle To Your Life

Principle #6: We Need To Embrace The Word Of God As Our Guide So We May Faithfully Live Out The Christian Life (2 Timothy 3:16-17)

1.   Ask yourself an honest question: why do I read my Bible? Craft a letter addressed to God and tell Him why. After all, He sent you 66 letters contained in two testaments in one volume. May I suggest you keep your letter to Him a bit shorter.

2.   What is your favorite book of Bible? What is your favorite passage of Scripture? Who is your favorite Bible character? What is your favorite Bible story?

3.   When you read from your Bible and God speaks to your heart, do you have a system where you can write down His promises, His comfort, His challenges to you?

A Prayer Of Application:

Lord Jesus, I desire to live above the fray. I want to embrace the Word of God as my guide so I may faithfully live out the Christian life.

Chapter Seven

Stay Focused!

Living Above The Fray Means We Keep The Main Thing,
The Main Thing

*Principle #7: We Need To Be Faithful And Do What God Has
Called And Equipped Us To Do For Him*
(2 Timothy 4:1-5)

"Remember that the power comes through you, not from you."
Fred Smith Sr.

*"Walk with me and work with me—watch how I do it. Learn the
unforced rhythms of grace.*
I won't lay anything heavy or ill-fitting on you.
Keep company with me and you'll learn to live freely and lightly"
Matthew 11:28-30 From The MESSAGE

There are many leaders today who fail to get the job
done. They do not finish well. Leadership professor Bobby
Clinton states in his book, *"The Making of a Leader"* that only
30 percent of leaders finish well. That piece of information is
disturbing on many levels. Looking at it another way, in a
room of ten leaders only three are going to be faithful to their
call as a leader and finish well. That means, for whatever
reasons, seven will not make the positive legacy cut. This is a

fact: some leaders will not finish well. They will turn to "inner idols" and suffer the fate of a wasted life. As I discussed in the first part of this book, Leader-I-Tis takes no mercy upon the proud, the fearful, or even the well-intentioned leader who is blind and oblivious to the danger of working in a toxic environment.

I am certain that any leader reading this book does not want to become one of the seventy percent who does not finish well. What are we to do to make certain that we will not fall into the trap of living to seek the approval from the leaders of the seventy percent? How can we resist the alluring bait of celebrating personality cults? How can we build a positive legacy that will last well beyond our brief time on earth? What steps can we take that will help us finish well? There are many books and multiple opinions on how this can be accomplished. Some are helpful. Many are not. I've chosen to seek the apostle Paul's advice given to his mentoree, Timothy. I suggest you do the same.

[1] I solemnly charge *you* in the presence of God and of Christ Jesus, who is to judge the living and the dead, and by His appearing and His kingdom: [2] preach the word; be ready in season *and* out of season; reprove, rebuke, exhort, with great patience and instruction. [3] For the time will come when they will not endure sound doctrine; but *wanting* to have their ears

tickled, they will accumulate for themselves teachers in accordance to their own desires, [4] and will turn away their ears from the truth and will turn aside to myths. [5] But you, be sober in all things, endure hardship, do the work of an evangelist, fulfill your ministry. **(2 Timothy 4:1-5)**

How to Create A Lasting Legacy

If you want to be a good leader, then there are at least eight leadership principles you must learn about and then faithfully live them out. I must warn you on the front-end. None of these are easy tasks. Yes, we need to embrace the grace of God in all that we do for Him. But He will not do it *for* us. If we are willing, He is more than willing do it *through* us. And that, my friends, makes all the difference in the world.

1. Preach the Word (vs. 2)
2. Be ready in season and out of season (vs. 2)
3. Reprove, rebuke, exhort, with great patience and instruction (vs. 2)
4. Don't be trapped by Group Think and the fear of man: It will lead you down a path of destruction called Leader-I-Tis (vs. 3-4)
5. Be sober in all things (vs. 5)
6. Endure hardship (vs. 5)
7. Do the work of an evangelist (vs. 5)

8. Fulfill your ministry [or your role as a Quality Leader] (vs. 5)

Preach the Word (vs. 2)

This might be one of the most misunderstood commands in the Bible. Many people too quickly conclude this applies only to their pastor or to the really "spiritual" people like Billy Graham. No, it applies to everyone who is a disciple of Jesus. But what does it mean to "preach the Word?" It does not always mean standing behind the protective covering of a pulpit or teaching lectern. More often than not, the proper application of this command is to "preach the Word" where you live, where you work, where you go and just as important, what you are facing as you seek to live above the fray.

To preach the Word means you are to proclaim it, to be a herald of it, to announce it. Preaching the Word is more than using words. It also includes how we choose to respond to things we do not like. What does it look like when you are fighting to live above the fray? Contrary to popular belief, the words of Jesus might surprise and even shock you.

When you are offended and treated unfairly, what are you to "preach" to yourself?

[38] "You have heard the law that says the punishment must match the injury: 'An eye for an eye, and a tooth for a tooth.' [39] But I say, do not resist an evil person! If someone slaps you on the right cheek, offer the other cheek also. [40] If you are sued in court and your shirt is taken from you, give your coat, too. [41] If a soldier demands that you carry his gear for a mile, carry it two miles. [42] Give to those who ask, and don't turn away from those who want to borrow. **Matthew 5:38-42 (NLT)**

When your enemies are against you, what are you to "preach" to yourself?

[43] "You have heard the law that says, 'Love your neighbor' and hate your enemy. [44] But I say, love your enemies! Pray for those who persecute you! [45] In that way, you will be acting as true children of your Father in heaven. For he gives his sunlight to both the evil and the good, and he sends rain on the just and the unjust alike. [46] If you love only those who love you, what reward is there for that? Even corrupt tax collectors do that much. [47] If you are kind only to your friends, how are you different from anyone else? Even pagans do that. **Matthew 5:43-47 (NLT)**

If you are going to be able to live above the fray, you are going to have to learn how to preach the Word, especially to yourself.

Be ready in season and out of season (vs. 2)

There are many people I know, including myself, who have a pocket full of "round-tuits." You know what I mean: One day I will take care of that project I've been putting off for a long time. When I am ready, then I will make that hard to make phone call to apologize for something I've done wrong. When the time is right, I'll take the time and study my Bible so I will know what I believe. We all have round-tuits. Its time to cash them in and not hoard them until the "right time" comes to give them away.

This was Paul's advice to Timothy: be ready because you never know when, and where, and with whom you will need to share the truth in a convincing way with those you come into contact. Here are a few things you can do in order to be ready.

1. *You need to be assured that God does love you*, without any strings attached. Some us have no problem that God loves others, but are hesitant that He loves "me." Believe me. No, believe Him, He does love you. If you and I are going to be able to live above the fray, we've got to know and experience His great love for us.

2. *You need to live in His grace.* It is always sufficient and it is always more than enough for you to take the next step and inhale the next breath in an extremely difficult

working environment. Grace will free you from having to be perfect and it will perfectly keep you from giving up while living above the fray.

3. *A heart of worship* will help you keep the main thing the main thing. When you are making a choice to worship Jesus in spite of how you are feeling, you are able to "float" above the toxic chaos below. Worship does not necessarily mean your problems go away, but it does mean you are better equipped to face them in a healthy way.

4. *Reading God's Word* gives you the opportunity to fill your heart with the principles that will change you from the inside out. Some have said reading and reflecting upon the Bible will replace your stinking thinking with words that are true. There are a thousand ways (reading plans, topical studies, book studies, etc.) to open up God's Word. Find what works best for you and do it. If you are going to successfully live above the fray, you are going to have to ground yourself in the Word.

5. *Prayer, talking to God and listening to God,* helps you be ready in season and out of season. Prayer is the lifeline of communication we have with God. If you fail to use it, often, you will often not be prepared when an opportunity He sends comes your way. When working in

a toxic organization, it is essential you keep the lines of communication open.

6. *Being a member of a healthy community* of like-minded friends helps you be ready. Accountability, positive peer pressure, is a wonderful tool that keeps everyone ready so they may follow through with agreed upon commitments. It has been said, it takes a village to raise a child. Even more so, it takes a group of trusted friends, allies of the heart, to give you the courage and inner fortitude to live above the fray. This statement is true: there is strength in numbers and the more people who have committed to watch your back will help you be ready in season and out of season. Yes, you will grow weary. Yes, you will want to give up. But yes, you can live above the fray because of the company you keep.

7. *Being a servant leader* is the antidote to looking within and feeling sorry for you. I am not discounting your personal grief and suffering. It is real and it is a part of the equation. However, once you can begin to free yourself to serve others, your perspective will change. If you are self-centered you will likely miss an opportunity to be ready in season (when its convenient to serve) and out of season (when its not convenient to serve).

8. *Share your faith.* The very meaning of the word "evangelism" means Good News. Good News is

especially important for those who work in toxic environments. You can be ready in season and out of season when you learn how to share your faith (the hope that lies within) with authenticity, not a canned, artificial presentation. A real faith gives you real credibility with real people who are in search for real answers.

> But in your hearts set apart Christ as Lord. Always be prepared to give an answer to everyone who asks you to give the reason for the hope that you have. But do this with gentleness and respect, **1 Peter 3:15 (NIV)**

Reprove, rebuke, exhort, with great patience and instruction (vs. 2)

If you are going to live above the fray and not be poisoned by Leader-I-Tis, you are going to have to be assertive, not passive. I know that this will be challenging for many of you. It is for me. My very nature is a passive one. I would much rather avoid a hard confrontation than to deal with it head on and see where the chips may land. I'm learning how to become more assertive when I need to be, but I've got a ways to go yet. But I am learning, and you can too.

Paul uses some strong words here to get the point across: Reprove, Rebuke, and Exhort. This sounds pretty confrontational to me, and it is. But notice how he tells

Timothy to do it: "with great patience and instruction." Lets take a look on how we can be confrontational but couple it with great patience and instruction.

To be patient is to be long-suffering. It is a word where grace can find a place to fit in. Patient people are people who are committed to the process that is required to bring them to the truth. That is where the instruction comes into play. The goal is not to bash people with reproof, rebukes and strong exhortations and end there. The goal is to move these people towards a place of learning, a place of change, a place of inner transformation. Yes, it does require patience, but when it works, it is well worth the wait.

The truth is the truth, but there are no guarantees on how this works out in your life. One of my regrets is that I was more committed to peace at any cost (passivity, misguided) than engaging in conflict. And for whatever reason, I failed to reprove, rebuke and exhort when I had the opportunity to be more assertive. I'm learning and I hope you will too. If we are going to live above the fray, we are going to have to become more assertive people.

Don't be trapped by Group Think and the fear of man: It will lead you down a path of destruction called Leader-I-Tis (vs. 3-4)

These are powerful words from Paul: "[3] For the time will come when they will not endure sound doctrine; but *wanting* to have their ears tickled, they will accumulate for themselves teachers in accordance to their own desires, [4] and will turn away their ears from the truth and will turn aside to myths." He predicts a time where the temptation to swallow a pack of lies lock, stock and barrel will overwhelm many. The time is now.

Group Think is when alternative ideas are not invited into the mindset of an organization's leadership. In the name of "unity" nothing outside the organization's "company line" is accepted. Group Think is why reasonable and intelligent people make disastrous decisions. Just as Paul claimed, there will be people who "will not endure sound doctrine; but *wanting* to have their ears tickled, they will accumulate for themselves teachers in accordance to their own desires, and will turn away their ears from the truth and will turn aside to myths."

It is this simple: a healthy organization invites a broad perspective of ideas. An organization infected by Leader-I-Tis shuns any idea but their own. It takes a brave leader to stand up to the powerful crowd and tell the truth. If you want to create a lasting legacy, then the best place to begin is to make the decision now to fear God more than man. This is a lesson

I should have learned long ago: it matters most what God says about you, not what others think about and say about you. The very moment you give into the fear of others, the hungry sharks smell your blood in the water and come after you.

Be sober in all things (vs. 5)

Paul uses an interesting word here. He is not saying don't overdo it on the wine. He is not saying don't allow this drink to become the way you cope with life. He is saying you need to keep your cool, stay alert and watchful; be sober in all things. When life's pressures come your way, what is your drug of choice? Is it too much wine, too much eating, too much shopping? I hope you get the point. This charge, to be sober in all things, has nothing to do with the abstention of or the wrong consumption of alcohol. It has everything to do with how you will be able to live above the fray when your circumstances demand you have a clear mind to think, to act, and even how to strategically pray.

Endure hardship (vs. 5)

This is one of the key principles of being able to live above the fray. More often than not, it requires of you and I to experience endurance during times of hardship. Sure, we wished that our challenges would be short and sweet. Don't we all? However, we have come to learn by our experiences that this type of wishful thinking has no basis in reality. I heard one of my seminary professors quote this phrase many times: *"Never raise the white flag of surrender during the smoke of battle."* How many battles have been lost, because of a premature surrender? How many people have become weary of the fight and quit trying to make a difference for Jesus at work? If you are committed to do what it takes to live above the fray, then you must endure hardship.

Do the work of an evangelist (vs. 5)

A word of clarity is needed here. Paul does not mean that everyone needs to have the same spiritual gift of the evangelist. What he does mean is everyone needs to do the *work* of an evangelist. What does that really look like? The Bible has a lot to say about evangelism, about the need of every believer to share the gospel, the good news, to the lost.

A.   We Are To Go And Make Disciples Of All Nations.

19Therefore go and make disciples of all nations, baptizing them in the name of the Father and of the Son and of the Holy Spirit, 20and teaching them to obey everything I have commanded you. And surely I am with you always, to the very end of the age." **Matthew 28:19-20 (NIV)**

***PERSONAL APPLICATION:

The call to the making of disciples is not limited to the pastor or professional Christian worker. NO, instead, the call is to EVERYONE who claims to have a relationship with Jesus Christ. We can learn and then apply several key points of how we are to relate to the world around us:

1. All of us are to GO and make disciples.
2. All of us are to make an impact of all nations—if we can't physically go, then assist those who can.
3. All of us are to encourage the disciples we make to identify with the Father, Jesus Christ, and the Holy Spirit.
4. All of us are to teach the disciples we make just how important obedience to the Lord's teachings are to those who follow Him.
5. All of us need to know that Jesus Christ is with us—every step of the way in this world in which we live.

One of the great opportunities that a quality disciple faces is the unfinished task of world evangelization. How is a person to gain a heart for the lost and dying souls of the world? He or she must have a heart for God and a desire to fulfill the Great Commission.

B.   Evangelism Was The Ministry Of Jesus Christ.

For the Son of Man came to seek and to save what was lost."
Luke 19:10 (NIV)

***PERSONAL APPLICATION:

All around us are people who are lost, who do not have a saving relationship with Jesus Christ. It is with a sense of gratitude that the disciple of Christ reaches out to those who need to hear the glorious message of the Cross—that Jesus Christ came and died and rose again for the forgiveness of sin.

The quality disciple has learned to look beyond him or herself and seek out those who are lost. There is a burden to share the life-changing Gospel with those who are in such desperate need. In today's culture, it is easy to become satisfied with one's own salvation, forgetting that for those who die without Christ will face an eternity cut off from the presence of God.

C.   Each Believer Needs To Be Willing, Eager To Share The Gospel.

^{14}I am obligated both to Greeks and non-Greeks, both to the wise and the foolish. ^{15}That is why I am so eager to preach the gospel also to you who are at Rome. [16]I am not ashamed of the gospel, because it is the power of God for the salvation of everyone who believes: first for the Jew, then for the Gentile. **Romans 1:14-16 (NIV)**

***PERSONAL APPLICATION:

Why is it that so many professing believers are hesitant to share their faith with an unbeliever? Sometimes the reason is that we are not convinced that the Gospel is powerful enough to save. *"I know that Christ saved me…but can He save THAT person?"* O, but the Gospel is powerful. In fact, the Gospel *is* the power of God for salvation.

The quality disciple is convinced that the message of the Gospel can change lives. While some would hesitate and be ashamed of such a strong conviction, the quality disciple is both willing and eager to share the Good News with any lost person that God sends his or her way.

D.   Each Believer Is Called To Do The Work Of An Evangelist, To Share The Good News Of The Gospel With The Lost.

But you, keep your head in all situations, endure hardship, do the work of an evangelist, discharge all the duties of your ministry. **2 Tim. 4:5 (NIV)**

***PERSONAL APPLICATION:

Not every believer is to assume the role of a traveling or professional evangelist, but every believer is called to do the *work* of an evangelist. And what is this work? It is doing whatever is required to bring a lost person to a saving knowledge of Jesus Christ.

Lost people do not come to the Lord by accident. Yes, it is the power and conviction of the Holy Spirit that leads a person to make a decision to receive Christ. But God does use His people to share the message that mankind is helpless and forever lost without Jesus Christ. The quality disciple is willing to do whatever it takes, to intentionally work towards bringing a lost soul to Christ.

E.   One Day, The Gospel Will Be Shared With The Entire World.

And the gospel must first be preached to all nations. **Mark 13:10 (NIV)**

6Then I saw another angel flying in midair, and he had the eternal gospel to proclaim to those who live on the earth--to every nation, tribe, language and people. 7He said in a loud voice, "Fear God and give him glory, because the hour of his judgment has come. Worship him who made the heavens, the earth, the sea and the springs of water." **Rev. 14:6-7 (NIV)**

***PERSONAL APPLICATION:

It is God who is in charge of this timeline, of when the Gospel will be shared with the entire world. But He has invited His disciples to join with Him for this great cause— that the world may know that Jesus Christ is Lord. He will do His part—will you? Taking the Gospel to the nations will happen one day. The quality disciple is intent on joining God and making sure that if it occurs this generation, he or she wants to be a part of this exciting time in history.

F.   The Ability To Evangelize Comes From The Power Of God.

[7]For God did not give us a spirit of timidity, but a spirit of power, of love and of self-discipline. [8]So do not be ashamed to testify about our Lord, or ashamed of me his prisoner. But join with me in suffering for the gospel, by the power of God, **2 Tim. 1:7-8 (NIV)**

***PERSONAL APPLICATION:

The life-changing Gospel was never meant to be shared using human strength. Instead, God has given us His power to share the message of salvation by grace, through faith. The quality disciple has discovered the secret to sharing his or her faith. Trusting in the power of God to give the right words and the right actions, the quality disciple experiences the joy of seeing God work in his or her life as the lost are saved and come to know Jesus Christ.

G.   The Ability To Evangelize Comes From The Holy Spirit.

7But I tell you the truth: It is for your good that I am going away. Unless I go away, the Counselor will not come to you; but if I go, I will send him to you. 8When he comes, he will convict the world of guilt in regard to sin and righteousness and judgment: 9in regard to sin, because men do not believe in me; 10in regard to righteousness, because I am going to the Father, where you can see me no longer; 11and in regard to judgment, because the prince of this world now stands condemned. **John 16:7-11 (NIV)**

But you will receive power when the Holy Spirit comes on you; and you will be my witnesses in Jerusalem, and in all Judea and Samaria, and to the ends of the earth." **Acts 1:8 (NIV)**

***PERSONAL APPLICATION:

Far too many people have tried to explain the Christian life to others without tapping into the power of the Holy Spirit. The promise of Scripture is clear to the believer: the power to an effective witness is intimately linked to having a relationship with the Holy Spirit. The math is simple: no power = no witness. The quality disciple is not willing to do God's work without having God's power.

H.   Every Believer Is To Share His Or Her Faith With The Lost.

He said to them, "Go into all the world and preach the good news to all creation. **Mark 16:15 (NIV)**

For the Son of Man came to seek and to save what was lost." **Luke 19:10 (NIV)**

Again Jesus said, "Peace be with you! As the Father has sent me, I am sending you." **John 20:21 (NIV)**

But you will receive power when the Holy Spirit comes on you; and you will be my witnesses in Jerusalem, and in all Judea and Samaria, and to the ends of the earth." **Acts 1:8 (NIV)**

But in your hearts set apart Christ as Lord. Always be prepared to give an answer to everyone who asks you to give the reason for the hope that you have. But do this with gentleness and respect, **1 Peter 3:15 (NIV)**

***PERSONAL APPLICATION:

There are some Christians who hesitate in sharing their faith because they might be misunderstood, or come across as being "intolerant" of the other person's beliefs. Nowhere in Scripture are there any instructions to avoid sharing your faith. Instead, the message is consistent: "Go into all the world...seek and save the lost...I am sending you...you will be my witnesses...be prepared to give an answer to everyone."

A little bit of personal preparation goes a long way in helping you present the Gospel in a clear way. If we are to truly be able to give an answer for the hope that we have, we need to know what that hope is and how to share it. This is exactly what the quality disciple is equipped to do.

I.   Why Are We To Evangelize? The Fields Are Ripe Unto Harvest With Souls That Need The Saving Message Of The Gospel.

Do you not say, 'Four months more and then the harvest'? I tell you, open your eyes and look at the fields! They are ripe for harvest. **John 4:35 (NIV)**

***PERSONAL APPLICATION:

Everyday people die and are lost forever. It is sobering to hear that unless workers are sent into the field, the crops, the souls of lost men, women, boys, and girls will be lost. In life we are presented with many opportunities. Some are taken advantage of and others are lost forever. The quality disciple refuses to squander the chance to go into God's field of lost souls and win them to Christ.

J.   Why Are We To Evangelize? It Is The Power Of God For The Salvation Of Everyone Who Believes.

I am not ashamed of the gospel, because it is the power of God for the salvation of everyone who believes: first for the Jew, then for the Gentile. **Romans 1:16 (NIV)**

***PERSONAL APPLICATION:

Some believers are cowered by the weight of peer pressure, not willing to go against the grain of popular culture. The Gospel is much too precious to be ashamed of. The shame is when a believer refuses to believe in the power of the Gospel to change lives. The quality disciple has moved beyond caring what other people think about his or her faith in the Gospel. A choice has been already made, a conviction already confirmed, that God's Word is absolutely true: the Gospel is the power of God for the salvation of everyone who believes.

K.   Why Are We To Evangelize? The Harvest Of Souls Is Plentiful.

He told them, "The harvest is plentiful, but the workers are few. Ask the Lord of the harvest, therefore, to send out workers into his harvest field. **Luke 10:2 (NIV)**

***PERSONAL APPLICATION:

One of the keys to world evangelization is to pray, to ask the Lord of the harvest to send workers, those who share the Gospel, into the harvest field of lost souls. Without a doubt, we would be much further along in the goal of reaching the nations if we would only sharpen our life of prayer. The quality disciple has made the decision to create a prayer strategy that will earnestly ask the Lord to send passionate believers to share the gospel into every nation on earth.

L.   We Are To Have Zeal, A Passion To Share The Gospel With Family And Friends Who Do Not Know The Lord.

9:1I speak the truth in Christ--I am not lying, my conscience confirms it in the Holy Spirit-- 2I have great sorrow and unceasing anguish in my heart. [3]For I could wish that I myself were cursed and cut off from Christ for the sake of my brothers, those of my own race, **Romans 9:1-3 (NIV)**

***PERSONAL APPLICATION:

One of the hardest mission fields is with the people who know you best. It is by far, the most challenging, but most rewarding experience when God uses you to lead a family member or close friend to Christ. Instead of running away from the opportunity, may God give you an ache in your heart, a burden that cannot be lifted until you make the decision to be a witness to your lost family and friends. It takes real courage to open your life to those who know you best; especially those who knew you before you invited Christ to take control of your life. The quality disciple is comfortable in reaching out to lost family members and close friends—no matter what they might think about him or her.

M.   We Need To Have The Same Intensity, If Not More So, To Win The Lost To Christ As Do Those Who Have A Sincere Passion To Persuade The Spiritually Blind To Follow Them.

"Woe to you, teachers of the law and Pharisees, you hypocrites! You travel over land and sea to win a single convert, and when he becomes one, you make him twice as much a son of hell as you are. **Matthew 23:15 (NIV)**

***PERSONAL APPLICATION:

It is important to note that you are not the only one seeking to evangelize someone. There are many, far too many, who prey upon the spiritually blind. These spiritual predators have passion, a sincere and devoted goal to lead the deceived down the road of destruction. A member of another faith should never outwork the Christian believer. The stakes are too costly to lose even one soul. The quality disciple understands that it is time to go to work, and to do so with passion and zeal. The battle for lost souls is too important to lose. Evangelism is not just a recreational activity for the believer—it must become a way of life.

It is true that when we have a burden, a passion to do something, we will do all we can to accomplish our goal. That same principle is true when it comes to sharing our faith with the lost. A passionate believer will be a passionate soul-winner. On the other hand, a believer who fails to capture God's burden for the lost, will be numb to the souls that fall into a Christ-less eternity. It is our duty; it is our great privilege to share the Good News of the Gospel of Jesus Christ.

Fulfill your role as a Quality Leader (vs. 5)

This verse underscores one of the most powerful themes in the Bible: being faithful to one's own calling. There are some "jobs" that someone else can do for you, but there is one job that only you can do: the job that God has given you to do. Lets briefly examine several different translations of this verse.

⁵ But you, be sober in all things, endure hardship, do the work of an evangelist, <u>fulfill your ministry</u>. **2 Timothy 4:5 (NASB)**

⁵ But as for you, be serious about everything, endure hardship, do the work of an evangelist, <u>fulfill your ministry</u>. **2 Timothy 4:5 (HCSB)**

⁵ But you, keep your head in all situations, endure hardship, do the work of an evangelist, <u>discharge all the duties of your ministry</u>. **2 Timothy 4:5 (NIV)**

⁵ But you should keep a clear mind in every situation. Don't be afraid of suffering for the Lord. Work at telling others the Good News, and <u>fully carry out the ministry God has given you</u>. **2 Timothy 4:5 (NLT)**

⁵ But *you*—keep your eye on what you're doing; accept the hard times along with the good; keep the Message alive; <u>do a thorough job as God's servant</u>. **2 Timothy 4:5 (MSG)**

The Greek word Paul chooses here for "fulfill, discharge, fully carry out, or do a thorough job," literally means to fill it to the brim. What a powerful word picture to show us what God expects from us as we serve Him. Too many of us have settled for half-full commitments that keep us from experiencing success. The reason for those who live below the fray and not above the fray is due mostly to the fact that they fail to fully maximize their opportunities by growing in their calling. In this case, Paul exhorts Timothy to fill to the brim something very specific. He did not say fill to the brim those things that only please you. He failed to say that Timothy should make an investment into the things that are superficial. No, Paul told to Timothy to fill to the brim his commitment to the ministry of service God has given him.

Here is the bottom line to all of this: our culture tells us that everything is about us. Everything and everyone (including God) has been placed on this earth to run and fetch for us. Unfortunately, this sense of entitlement even runs amuck with some church leaders. Listen carefully to what Paul told Timothy about his ministry. He did not say that the reason for his ministry was to make Timothy feel good and have his ministry fulfill him. But this is the very real experience of many leaders today: "what can you and this organization do for me so I will feel better about myself?" Instead, this exhortation from Paul to Timothy is in stark contrast in that it cuts across the grain of what we have been taught to expect. Instead of our ministries fulfilling us, we should be about the business of fulfilling them. The first perspective places the focus upon us. The second perspective places the focus upon the right One. To successfully live above the fray, you've got to know what God has called you to do and then fully invest yourself into fulfilling your call.

Jesus has invested a lot in you. He has saved you, strengthened you, and in Paul's experience, was found to be faithful enough in order to be used in His Kingdom. In response for all He has done for you, what will you invest in Him?

I thank Christ Jesus our Lord, who has strengthened me, because He considered me faithful, putting me into service, **1 Timothy 1:12 (NASB)**

In conclusion, here is the take-a-way for those who desire to live above the fray. You will be successful if you know who you are and know what God has called you to do for Him. Living above the fray does not just happen by accident. Living above the fray has nothing to do with luck. Living above the fray does not happen just because you know who you are and you know what God has called you to do. To live above the fray and thrive requires you to stay focused and to live like you know who you are and then apply what you know to do. Then, and only then, will you be able to say with a confident assurance: I have learned how to not only survive but also to thrive when serving in a toxic organization.

Summary:

If you want to live above the fray then . . . **Stay Focused!** You Need To Be Faithful And Do What God Has Called And Equipped You To Do For Him

Reflect and Respond

Apply This Principle To Your Life

Principle #7: We Need To Be Faithful And Do What God Has Called And Equipped Us To Do For Him (2 Timothy 4:1-5)

1.   A legacy does not begin a few moments before your death. Your legacy takes years for your story and your character and your contribution to others to make an impact worth remembering. Have you ever wanted to know what your family, friends, and peers will say at your funeral? Take some time and write the script you want to hear from them.

2.   There are at least eight leadership principles mentioned in this chapter. Of the eight, which one is your strongest one? Why? Which one is your greatest opportunity for growth? What is your strategy to grow in this area?

3.   In what ways are you purposing in your heart to live above the fray?

A Prayer Of Application:

Lord Jesus, I desire to live above the fray. I want to be faithful and do what You have called and equipped me to do for You.

Epilogue: Revisiting The Boardroom

The rest of the story:

The Boardroom is where the ten men who were infected by Leader-I-Tis used to hold court. What was once a mighty kingdom came crashing down, leaving the organization a shell of its former self. A boardroom of a deathly sick organization can be representative of the fatal impact Leader-I-Tis can have upon an organization and its leaders. If the room could speak, there would be many sad and tragic stories of leadership failure.

The posters on the wall are full of the next great ideas intended to save the organization from ruin. The trashcan is filled with crumpled-up papers of desperate measures that required rewrite after rewrite. The reverberating echoes in the room grow quieter as the angry speeches and spirited debates fade away into a muted hush. The harder the board tried, the worse it got. No matter what the board did, or believed, the ship still sank. To the very end, they remained in denial as they commanded the musicians to keep on playing and spent precious time rearranging the deck chairs. Many lives were lost. Not as in a physical dying, but maybe a fate even worse: precious time was lost, reputations were shattered, dreams became nightmares, families were divided, and what was once a shining example of a healthy organization crashed and burned into a smoldering heap of "what could have been."

Acute Leader-I-Tis has a way of causing leaders to go stone deaf and blind. One could have reasonably hoped that the leadership board would have come to their senses and rallied to the cause and freed themselves from this organizational disease. But it was not meant to be: they were infected and had become a part of the problem of Leader-I-Tis. That's the funny thing about this disease. It has a way of numbing you and killing you without you even knowing it.

Every leader is given the choice: to allow this hideous disease to infect and sicken them, or find a way to survive and perhaps even thrive while serving in a toxic organization. Certainly, we want to be of help. Quality Leaders really desire to be a part of a team that would help a once great organization return to good health. Perhaps you have hung in there hoping against hope. Maybe you should have thrown up your hands in disgust and walked away years ago. Many of us are loyal, often to a fault. But we really want to help.

I wish I had the kind of story that would really impress you of my great leadership skills. Sorry. I found my set of circumstances over the past thirty years to be some of my greatest personal challenges. I became discouraged and even depressed. At times, I felt I had lost my way. I am a leader and I should have known better and done better. And

I am human. But listen carefully to what I say: my failure and your failure to do it perfectly does not negate the truth of the seven principles I have shared with you about how to live above the fray and even thrive as you do so. If you commit to Stay Useful, Stay Strategic, Stay Alert, Stay Strong, Stay Connected, Stay Grounded, and Stay Focused the chances are you will find many successes in your life's journey.

Because I am a Christ-follower I am a life-long advocate of the grace of God. His grace does things I cannot do on my own . . . like to live above the fray and thrive along the way.

[12] I don't mean to say that I have already achieved these things or that I have already reached perfection. But I press on to possess that perfection for which Christ Jesus first possessed me. [13] No, dear brothers and sisters, I have not achieved it, but I focus on this one thing: Forgetting the past and looking forward to what lies ahead, [14] I press on to reach the end of the race and receive the heavenly prize for which God, through Christ Jesus, is calling us. **Philippians 3:12-14 (NLT)**

I have chosen to keep on pressing on. I hope you will too.

Subject Index

Alert
Duty. To stay a. Pg. 60

Anderson, Dr. Morris
Characteristics of a mentor. Pg. 83
        Approachable. Pg. 83
        Challenging call to live a significant life. Pg. 83
        Empowers others to minister. Pg. 83
        Father figure. Pg. 83

Appreciate – Appreciation
Failure to a and praise others. Pg. 10
        Example of. Pg. 38

Argue – Arguing – Argument
Fact. It is possible to win the argument but lose the relationship. Pg. 62

Arrogant – Arrogance
Danger of. Can slip into a based upon past success. Pg. 68
Fact.
        Sees himself as better than anyone else. Pg. 73
        Uses other people to get what he wants. Pg. 73
Meaning of. Pg. 73

Assert – Assertive
Fact. If we are going to live above the fray, we are going to have to be more a. Pg. 117

Barnabus
Mentored Paul. Pg. 94

Be Ready In Season And Out Of Season
Duty. Get rid of your round-tuits. Pg. 114
Meaning of. Pg. 114

Be Ready In Season And Out Of Season (continued)
Preparation to be ready. 8 action steps. Pg. 114

Bible Study
Accessible in many different formats. Pg. 97
Benefits of.
> Are able to discern what other people say is either true or false. Pg. 100, 103
> Are challenged not only to read the Bible but to hear it and take it to heart. Pg. 100
> Are encouraged and promised an inheritance. Pg. 100, 102
> Are taught, rebuked, corrected, and trained in righteousness. Pg. 102
> Can prove that Jesus is the Christ, the risen Savior, the Son of God. Pg. 100, 103
> Find instruction concerning endurance, encouragement and hope. Pg. 99, 102
> Gain assurance of eternal life and answered prayer. Pg. 99, 101
> Learn how to correctly handle the word of truth. Pg. 100, 103

Duty.
> Must apply what you are reading. Pg. 97
> Must stay grounded in God's Word. Pg. 96, 98, 107

Fact.
> A proper understanding and practical application of grace and worship is critical when it comes to the core value of Bible study. Pg. 99
> Goal of Bible study. Pg. 98
> God does speak to us through His Word. Pg. 96
> Need His help to understand the Scriptures. Pg. 105
> Spiritual formation cannot and will not take place without significant and consistent participation in God's Word. Pg. 96

Bible Study (continued)

How to study: Four steps

Observation: What is the author saying? Pg. 97

Interpretation: What does it mean? Pg. 97

Application: What does it mean to me? Pg. 97

Proclamation: What does it mean through me? Pg. 97

Relationship Driven. Pg. 96, 99

Results of.

Assurance of eternal life and answered prayer. Pg. 99, 101

Can prove that Jesus is the Christ. Pg. 100, 103

Encouraged and promised an inheritance. Pg. 102

Finds instruction concerning endurance, encouragement and hope. Pg. 99, 102

Learns how to discern what is true and false. Pg. 100, 103

Learns how to handle correctly the word of truth. Pg. 99, 100, 103, 106

Produces change. Pg. 96, 100, 115

Takes it to heart. Pg. 100, 102

Taught, rebuked, corrected, and trained in righteousness. Pg. 100, 102

Techniques. Pg. 97, 98

Need the help of other teachers when we are uncertain of the meaning. Pg. 105

Need the help of the Holy Spirit. Pg. 105

Need to be a diligent workman in the Scriptures. Pg. 106

Need to compare Scripture with Scripture. Pg. 105

Need to study the Scriptures everyday. Pg. 98, 103, 107

Boast – Boastful – Boasting

Fact. Talks big but rarely has anything to show for it. Pg. 73

Meaning of. Pg. 73

Warning. No one should boast. Pg. 50

Brutal
Fact. Has no conscience and derives a sick pleasure in hurting other people, deeply. Pg. 75
Meaning of. 75

Bully – Bullying (See also Spiritual Bullies, Workplace Bullying)
Characteristics of.
      18 qualities. Pg. 73
      Are often surrounded by their protective entourage. Pg. 71
      Use their power to manipulate others to get their way. Pg. 70
Example of. Kind of. Workplace. Pg. 61
Warning.
      Are not only confined to the playground. Pg. 70
      Spiritual bullying can cause great harm and it needs to be exposed. Pg. 71
      We need to beware of them. Pg. 68

Call – Calling
As a prayer. To call on the Lord. Pg. 57
      How. From a pure heart. Pg. 57
Supersedes an extraordinary skill or popularity. Pg. 13

Challenge
Failure to make strategic adjustments during a historic c. Pg. 12, 23

Change
Quote. Tolstoy. Pg. 43

Chemistry
Failure to build a team that has great c. Pg. 12, 28

Clean – Cleansing
Benefits of. Pg. 45
Dangers of not being c. Pg. 44
Fact. Cleansing agent is grace. Pg. 47
Meaning of. Pg. 44
Promises of. Pg. 44, 47

Clinton, Bobby
Leadership professor says only 30% of leaders finish well. Pg. 109

Communicate – Communication
Failure to c in a clear and convincing way. Pg. 11, 24
Lack of. Example of. Pg. 24

Conceit – Conceited
Fact. The conceited person is destroyed by success. Pg. 76
Meaning of. Pg. 76

Confront – Confrontation
How to. With great patience and instruction. Pg. 111, 117, 118

Connect – Connected
Duty. We need to seek out mentors who live out what they teach and believe. Pg. 82

Dangerous People
Characteristics of. 18 qualities. Pg. 71

Deviant Doctrines
Example of. The personality cult. Pg. 71

Difficult People
Challenge. Need to learn how to effectively relate to them. Pg. 60
Characteristics of. 18 qualities. Pg. 71

Difficult Times
Fact. In the last days difficult times will come. Pg. 72

Discussion
Failure to create a safe place for. Pg. 9
      Example of. Pg. 34

Disobedient To Parents
Fact. If rebellion thrives in the home then no society is safe from its toxic poison. Pg. 74
Meaning of. Pg. 74

Empower – Empowerment
Failure to help others reach their full potential. Pg. 11, 35, 36
Prayer of. To be a good mentor. Pg. 95
Through grace. Pg. 92
To serve. Pg. 84

Endure Hardship
Duty. Must endure. Pg. 111, 120
Fact.
      All leaders go through hardship. Pg. 120
      Some surrender and give up. Pg. 121
      To be a quality leader must be able to endure hardship. Pg. 134

Entitle – Entitlement
Fact.
      Spiritual narcissists feel entitled because of their position. Pg. 69
      The ungrateful person thinks he is entitled. Pg. 74

Evangelism – Evangelist – Evangelize
Fact.
      Evangelism was the ministry of Jesus. Pg. 123
      Everyone needs to share the gospel. Pg. 121, 123

Evangelism – Evangelist – Evangelize (continued)
One day the gospel will be shared with the entire world. Pg. 125, 126
The ability to evangelize comes from the Holy Spirit. Pg. 127
The ability to evangelize comes from the power of God. Pg. 126
Meaning of. Good news. Pg. 116
Responsibilities.
Each believer is called to do the work of an evangelist. Pg. 111, 121, 124, 125, 134
Each believer is to share his or her faith with the lost. Pg. 124, 128
Each believer needs to be willing, eager to share the gospel. Pg. 123, 124
We are to go and make disciples of all nations. Pg. 121
We are to have zeal, a passion to share the gospel with family and friends. Pg. 131
We need to have the same intensity to win the lost to Christ as does the Pharisee. Pg. 132
Why are we to evangelize?
It is the power of God for the salvation of everyone who believes. Pg. 124, 130
The fields are ripe unto harvest. Pg. 129
The harvest of souls is plentiful. Pg. 131

Example
Failure to lead by. Pg. 9
Example of. Pg. 30

Experience
Fact. Guided experience is the best guide in life. Pg. 82

Fair – Fairness
Fact. Life is not fair. Pg. 60

Faith
Duty. We are to pursue. Pg. 56
Fact.

A faith built on presumption will *disappoint*. Pg. 89
A faith built upon the truth of Jesus will *deliver*. Pg. 90
A faith that is built upon wrong belief will *deceive*. Pg. 90

Fear
Kind of. Fear of man. Pg. 111, 118
Warning. Will bring great harm to an organization. Pg. 15

Focus – Focused
Duty.

We need to be faithful and do what God has called and equipped us to do for Him. Pg. 109, 137, 138
Eight resources that will help you stay focused.

Community. Pg. 116
God's love. Pg. 114
God's Word. Pg. 115
Grace. Pg. 114
Prayer. Pg. 115
Serving. Pg. 116
Share (evangelism). Pg. 116
Worship. Pg. 115
Fact. Living above the fray means we keep the main thing the main thing. Pg. 109

Follow
Meaning of. Pg. 88

Follow My Conduct
Meaning of. Pg. 88

Follow My Faith
Meaning of. Pg. 89

Follow My Love
Meaning of. Pg. 90

Follow My Patience
Meaning Of. Pg. 90

Follow My Persecutions And Sufferings
Meaning Of. Pg. 92

Follow My Perseverance
Meaning Of. Pg. 91

Follow My Purpose
Meaning of. Pg. 89

Follow My Teaching
Meaning of. Pg. 88

Fulfill
Duty. To fulfill your role as a Quality Leader. Pg. 80
Meaning of. Pg. 112, 134

Future
Failure to plan for. Pg. 26
       Example of. Pg. 35
       Leaders who were to prepared. Pg. 10, 14, 36

Gentle – Gentleness
Benefits of. Pg. 65
Duty. Must with gentleness correct those who are in opposition. Pg. 64

Godliness
Holding to a form of g. Meaning of. Pg. 77

Good News
Duty. Need to share. Pg. 121, 133
Directed towards. The lost. Pg. 124
Fact. Evangelism means Good News. Pg. 116
Purpose of. Pg. 77

Good Work
Duty. To be prepared for every good work. Pg. 44, 50

Grace
Duty. Must learn the unforced rhythms of grace. Pg. 109

Grounded
Benefit of. Will be able to live above the fray. Pg. 107
Duty. Must stay grounded in God's Word. Pg. 96, 98

Group Think
Affects of. Danger of.
    Allows political correctness to run amuck. Pg. 69
    Alternative ideas are not heard. Pg. 119
    Causes reasonable and intelligent people to make disastrous decisions. Pg. 119
    Will lead you down a path of destruction called Leader-I-Tis. Pg. 118
Meaning of. Pg. 119

Gutenberg
Fact. Changed the world as we know it. Pg. 96
Inventor of the printing press. Pg. 96

Hater of Good
Fact. Despises people who embody goodness. Pg. 75
Meaning of. Pg. 75

Heart
Kind of. A pure heart. Pg. 57
       Meaning of. Pg. 57
       Source. Pg. 57

Higgins, Dr. Rick
Characteristics of a mentor. Pg. 84
       Advisor. Pg. 85
       Builds authentic relationships. Pg. 85
       Cheerleader. Pg. 85
       Friend. Pg. 85
       Is a safe place. Pg. 85
       Lives out what he believes. Pg. 85

Holy Spirit
Fact. Need His help to understand the Scriptures. Pg. 105

Humble – Humility
Benefits of. Makes us real. Pg. 68

Idol – Idolatry
Affects.
       Deludes others. Pg. 71
       Makes everyone sick. Pg. 17
Example of. Personality cult. Pg. 46

Imagination
Quote by Mark Twain. Pg. 3

Intention – Intentional
Duty.
       Must be I in actions and in right relationships. Pg. 52
       To bring a lost soul to Christ. Pg. 125

Irreconcilable
Fact. This person makes a commitment but breaks his word.
Pg. 74

Irreconcilable (continued)
Meaning of. Pg. 74

Kind – Kindness
Duty. Must be kind to all. Pg. 63
Meaning of. Pg. 63

Last Days
Fact.

In the last days difficult times will come. Pg. 72
People will be marked by 18 negative qualities. Pg. 72

Leader-I-Tis
Danger of.

Can cause leaders to go stone deaf and blind. Pg. 141
Failure to take responsibility. Pg. 20
Fear of rejection. Pg. 24
Is a people pleaser. Pg. 26
Numbs normally good leaders into a stupor. Pg. 22
Will infect others. Pg. 13
Will drain the life out of the organization. Pg. 16

Description of. Pg. 4
Early Symptoms of. Pg. 12

Fear to change the status quo. Pg. 13
Growing separation. Pg. 13
Lack of a commitment to take on the hard issues. Pg. 14
Leading out of fear and intimidation. Pg. 15
Self-serving ambition of the leader. Pg. 13

Meaning of. Pg. 4

Leadership
12 L failures that will sink an organization. Pg. 9
Leadership professor says only 30% of leaders finish well. Pg. 109
Legacy. How to create a lasting. Pg. 111
How to finish well. Pg. 111

Legacy
How to create a lasting. Eight leadership principles. Pg. 111
    Be ready in season and out of season. Pg. 114
    Be sober in all things. Pg. 120
    Do the work of an evangelist. Pg. 121
    Don't be trapped by Group Think and the fear of
man. Pg. 118
    Endure hardship. Pg. 120
    Fulfill your ministry [or role as a Quality Leader]. Pg.
134
    Preach the Word. Pg. 112
    Reprove, rebuke, exhort, with great patience and
instruction. Pg. 117
Warning. Some will not make the positive legacy cut. Pg. 109

Living Above The Fray
Fact. Does not happen by accident. Pg. 136

Love
Duty. We are to pursue. Pg. 56

Lover Of Pleasure Rather Than A Lover Of God
Fact. We place more value on the temporal than the eternal.
Pg. 76
Meaning of. Pg. 76

Malicious Gossip
Fact. Uses words to destroy with his tongue. Pg. 75
Meaning of. Pg. 75

Manage – Management
Failure to know the difference between managing programs
and leading people. Pg. 10
    Example of. Pg. 29

Master
Joy of the disciple. To be useful to Him. Pg. 49

McKechnie, Dr. Al
Characteristics of a mentor. Pg. 86
        Cheerleader. Pg. 86
        Encourager. Pg. 86
        Life coach. Pg. 86
        Present. Pg. 86

Mentor – Mentoring
Challenge:
        Who are you mentoring? Pg. 94
        Who are your spiritual leaders? Pg. 94
Characteristics of a mentor.
        Advisor. Pg. 85
        Approachable. Pg. 83
        Builds authentic relationships. Pg. 85
        Calls others to a life of worship and humility. Pg. 84
        Challenging call to live a significant life. Pg. 83
        Cheerleader. Pg. 85, 86
        Empowers others to minister. Pg. 83
        Empowers others to serve. Pg. 84
        Encourager. Pg. 86
        Father figure. Pg. 83
        Friend. Pg. 85
        Is a safe place. Pg. 85
        Life coach. Pg. 86
        Lives out what he believes. Pg. 85
        Present. Pg. 86
        Sacrificial giving. Pg. 83
Paul's example. Pg. 88
Duty. We need to seek out mentors who live out what they teach and believe. Pg. 82
Example of.
        Anderson, Dr. Morris. Pg. 83
        Barnabus. Pg. 94
        Higgins, Dr. Rick. Pg. 84
        McKechnie, Dr. Al. Pg. 85

Mentor – Mentoring (continued)
Paul. Pg. 87
Sherer, Knox. Pg. 83
Fact.
A good mentor knows what he or she believes and is able to clearly explain the truth to the mentoree. Pg. 82
Diversity is a great thing when it comes to mentoring. Pg. 86
Everyone needs to have a good mentor. Pg. 82, 95
Every Paul needs a Timothy. Pg. 94
Every Timothy needs a Paul. Pg. 94
Living above the fray requires good mentors. Pg. 82
Failure to invest in future leaders. Pg. 10
Example of. Pg. 14, 36
Legacy. Pg. 111
Responding to persecution: Role of mentors when I am undergoing persecution. Pg. 92

Momentum
Failure to capture the moment and build energy and m. Pg. 11
Kind of.
Negative. Pg. 8
Spiritual. Pg. 45

Money, Love of
Fact. Is a hoarder of money. Pg. 73
Meaning of. Pg. 73

Narcissist – Narcissism
Dangers of. Pg. 69
Description of. Pg. 69
Kind of. Spiritual. Pg. 69, 70
Warning. Do not become one. Pg. 70

Narcissus
Story of. Pg. 68

Organization
Fact. Every O life cycle has a peak. Pg. 8

Past
Failure to learn from. Pg. 9
       Example of. Pg. 31

Patient – Patience
Duty.
       Must be patient when wronged. Pg. 64
       Reprove, rebuke, and exhort with great p. Pg. 111,
117
Benefits of. Pg. 64
Meaning of. Follow my patience. Pg. 90
Qualities of patient people. Pg. 63

Paul
Charge to Timothy.
       Eight characteristics of living the Christian life. Pg. 88
Mentored by. Barnabus (the son of Encouragement). Pg. 94

Peace
Duty. We are to pursue. Pg. 56

Pen
Fact. Is mightier than the sword. Pg. 68

Persecution
Role of mentors during persecution. Pg. 92
Warning. All who desire to live godly in Christ Jesus will be
persecuted. Pg. 87, 93

Perseverance
Meaning Of. Pg. 91

Personality Cults
Consequences.

Personality Cults (continued)
Deludes others. Pg. 71
Makes everyone sick. Pg. 17
How to resist. Pg. 110

Potential
Failure to empower members to reach their full potential. Pg. 11, 35
Example of. Pg. 36

Power
Fact. Remember that the power comes through you, not from you. Pg. 109

Prayer
Answered. Pg. 79
Duty.
Must pray for others. Pg. 79
Must pray for yourself. Pg. 79
Example of David. Pg. 58
How to.
With a pure heart. Pg. 58

Preach The Word
Duty. Preach to yourself. Pg. 112
Meaning of. Pg. 112

Pride
Warning. Makes us artificial. Pg. 68

Prepare – Preparation
Duty.
To be prepared for every good work. Pg. 50
To give an answer for your hope. Pg. 117, 128, 129
Warning. If you do not pray, you will not be prepared. Pg. 115

Pure
Meaning of. Pg. 57
Type of heart. Pg. 57

Purpose
Fact. We have purpose for Kingdom affairs. Pg. 49
Meaning of. Pg. 49
Paul's charge. To follow my purpose. Meaning of. Pg. 89
To be useful to the Master. Pg. 49

Pursue – Pursuing
Duty.
    We need to be purposeful in *what* we pursue and with *whom* we pursue it. Pg. 52
    What we are to p. Pg. 55
List of what we are to pursue.
    Righteousness. Pg. 56
    Faith. Pg. 56
    Love. Pg. 56
    Peace. Pg. 56
Meaning of. Pg. 56

Quarrel – Quarrels – Quarrelsome
Caused by. Foolish and ignorant speculations. Pg. 62
Duty. We must not be Q. Pg. 63
Meaning of. Pg. 62, 63

Reckless
Fact.
    Great harm often comes to the organization a reckless person leads. Pg. 76
    Thinks only of himself. Pg. 76
Meaning of. Pg. 75

Repent – Repentance
Benefits. Transformation. Pg. 65
Of those who oppose us. Pg. 64

Reviler
Fact. We can blaspheme God when we insult others. Pg. 74
Meaning of. Pg. 73

Righteous – Righteousness
Duty.
       We are to be trained in it. Pg. 100, 102
       We are to pursue. Pg. 56
Meaning of. Pg. 56

Round-Tuits
Meaning of. Pg. 114

Sanctify – Sanctified
Illustration of.
       That person sanctifies me. Pg. 60
Meaning of. Pg. 48

Self-control, Without
Fact. Is out of control. Pg. 75
Meaning of. Pg. 75

Self, Lover of
Fact. It is the ultimate form of idolatry. Pg. 73
Meaning of. Pg. 73

Sherer, Knox
Characteristics of a mentor. Pg. 83
      Sacrificial giving. Pg. 83
      Empowered others to serve. Pg. 84
      Called others to a life of worship and humility. Pg. 84

Sin
Forgiveness of.
      Example of David. Pg. 57
      Example of John. Pg. 58

Sober
Benefits of. Pg. 120
Duty. Be sober in all things. Pg. 120
Meaning of. Pg. 120

Speculation – Speculations
Duty. Refuse foolish and ignorant s̲. Pg. 62
      Results of engaging in. Produces quarrels. Pg. 62

Spiritual Bondage
Freedom from. Pg. 65

Spiritual Bullies (See also Bully, Workplace Bullies)
Characteristics of. 18 qualities. Pg. 73
Warning.
      Some will always be under their influence. Pg. 80
      We need to beware of them. Pg. 68

Spiritual Formation
Fact.
      Does not come naturally to the believer. Pg. 101
      Spiritual formation cannot and will not take place
without significant and consistent participation in God's
Word. Pg. 100

Strategic Planning
Duty.
      Must be intentional in actions and in right
relationships. Pg. 36
      Must stay strategic. Pg. 52
Example of. Pg. 23
Failure to make s̲ adjustments during a historic challenge. Pg.
12, 23

Strong
Duty. Stay strong. Pg. 68

Submit – Submission
Warning. Egos, submitted to the Lordship of Jesus will bring great harm. Pg. 18
Wrong use of. Pg. 46

Success
Fact. Some handle success well. Others do not. Pg. 76
Failure to praise others for organization's s. Pg. 10
      Example of. Pg. 38
Warning. The conceited person is destroyed by success. Pg. 76

Surrender
Fact. Some face hardship and give up prematurely. Pg. 121

Teach – Teaching
Duty. Must be able to teach. Pg. 64
Meaning of. Pg. 64
Warning. False teaching. Pg. 46

Team - Teamwork
Failure to build a t that has great chemistry. Pg. 12
      Example of. Pg. 28

Transition
Fact.
      Refusal to create a culture of leadership transition will cripple an organization. Pg. 14
      The best time to leave an unhealthy toxic relationship. Pg. 50

Treacherous
Fact. Leaves a trusting person unprotected and betrays them. Pg. 75
Meaning of. Pg. 75

Turning of the Other Cheek
Example of. Pg. 61

Ungrateful
Fact. The ungrateful person thinks he is entitled to what he has been given. Pg. 74
Meaning of. Pg. 74

Unholy
Fact. Has no sense of decency. Pg. 74
Meaning of. Pg. 74

Unloving
Fact. This person is stoic and without human emotion. Pg. 74
Meaning of. Pg. 74

Useful
Duty. To stay clean and useful. Pg. 43
To the Master. Pg. 44, 49
        Meaning of. Pg. 44, 49

Woodstock
History of. Pg. 52

Workplace Bullying (See also Bully – Bullying)
Characteristics of. 18 qualities. Pg. 73
Example of. Pg. 31, 61
Fact. Seek to intimidate others. Pg. 70
Warning. We need to beware of them. Pg. 68

Youthful Lusts
Duty. To flee from. Pg. 53
Examples of. Pg. 54
Meaning of. Pg. 54

Scripture Index

Psalms
51:10. Pg. 58
115:1. Pg. 50

Proverbs
21:5. Pg. 76
25:14. Pg. 73

Isaiah
53:6. Pg. 165

Jeremiah
29:11. Pg. 165

Ezekiel
36:25. Pg. 47

Matthew
5:38-39. Pg. 61-62
5:38-42. Pg. 113
5:43-47. Pg. 113
6:33. Pg. 76
11:28-30. Pg. 109
23:12. Pg. 73
23:15. Pg. 132-133
28:19-20. Pg. 121

Mark
13:10. Pg. 125
16:15. Pg. 128

Luke
10:2. Pg. 131
19:10. Pg. 76, 122, 128

John
1:12-13. Pg. 166
1:29. Pg. 166
3:16. Pg. 166
4:35. Pg. 129
14:26. Pg. 105
15:2-3. Pg. 47
16:7-11. Pg. 127
20:21. Pg. 128
20:31. Pg. 100, 103

Romans
1:14-16. Pg. 124
1:16. Pg. Pg. 130
3:23. Pg. 165
6:12. Pg. 75
6:23. Pg. 165
9:1-3. Pg. 132
12:6-11. Pg. 14
12:9-10. Pg. 74
15:4. Pg. 99, 102

Acts
1:8. Pg. 127-128
8:30-38. Pg. 106
17:2-3. Pg. 103
17:11. Pg. 100, 103, 107
18:28. Pg. 100, 103
20:30. Pg. 71
20:32. Pg. 100, 102

1 Corinthians
1:2. Pg. 48
1:30. Pg. 49
2:13. Pg. 105
4:2. Pg. 49

2 Corinthians
7:1. Pg. 47
11:23-29. Pg. 91-92

Galatians
6:3. Pg. 76

Ephesians
2:8-10. Pg. 50
4:25. Pg. 74
4:32. Pg. 75
6:1-3. Pg. 74

Philippians
3:10. Pg. 92
3:12-14. Pg. 142

Colossians
3:16-17. Pg. 42

1 Thessalonians
4:9-10. Pg. 90
5:18. Pg. 74
5:23. Pg. 49

1 Timothy
1:12. Pg. 49, 136
6:10. Pg. 73

2 Timothy
1:7-8. Pg. 126
2:2. Pg. 49. 87
2:15. Pg. 99, 100, 103, 106
2:20-21. Pg. 43, 44, 51
2:22. Pg. 52, 53, 59
2:23-26. Pg. 60, 62, 67

3:1-9. Pg. 68, 72, 81
3:5. Pg. 76
3:10-15. Pg. 82, 87, 95
3:16. Pg. 100, 102
3:16-17. Pg. 96, 98, 108
4:1-5. Pg. 109, 111, 138
4:5. Pg. 124, 134
4:6-8. Pg. 49-50

Titus
1:8. Pg. 75

Hebrews
2:11. Pg. 48

James
3:3-12. Pg. 74
3:8-9. Pg. 74
4:17. Pg. 75

1 Peter
1:15. Pg. 48
3:15. Pg. 117, 128-129

2 Peter
3:11. Pg. 74

1 John
1:9. Pg. 48, 58
3:17. Pg. 73
5:13-15. Pg. 99, 101-102

Revelation
1:3. Pg. 100, 102
14:6-7. Pg. 125-126

HOW YOU CAN HAVE A RELATIONSHIP WITH JESUS

✓ GOD LOVES YOU AND HAS A WONDERFUL PLAN FOR YOUR LIFE

For I know the plans I have for you," declares the LORD, "plans to prosper you and not to harm you, plans to give you hope and a future. **Jeremiah 29:11 (NIV)**

✓ AS A RESULT OF MAN GOING HIS OWN WAY AND REJECTING GOD, A CHASM, A GREAT DIVIDE, HAS COME SEPARATING A JUST AND HOLY GOD FROM SINFUL MAN

for all have sinned and fall short of the glory of God, **Romans 3:23 (NIV)**

For the wages of sin is death, but the gift of God is eternal life in Christ Jesus our Lord. **Romans 6:23 (NIV)**

✓ GOD SENT HIS SON, HIS PERFECT SON TO BECOME OUR SACRIFICE. HE WHO IS SINLESS TOOK UPON HIMSELF OUR SINS, OFFERING TO RESTORE OUR BROKEN RELATIONSHIP WITH GOD, BRIDGING THE GAP BETWEEN GOD AND MAN

We all, like sheep, have gone astray, each of us has turned to his own way; and the LORD has laid on him the iniquity of us all. **Isaiah 53:6 (NIV)**

The next day John saw Jesus coming toward him and said, "Look, the Lamb of God, who takes away the sin of the world! **John 1:29 (NIV)**

✓ GOD HAS GIVEN EACH MAN A CHOICE EITHER TO ACCEPT THE FREE GIFT OF SALVATION AND LIVE FOREVER OR TO REJECT HIS GRACIOUS GIFT AND SPEND ETERNITY FOREVER SEPARATED FROM GOD

"For God so loved the world that he gave his one and only Son, that whoever believes in him shall not perish but have eternal life. **John 3:16 (NIV)**

12Yet to all who received him, to those who believed in his name, he gave the right to become children of God--
13children born not of natural descent, nor of human decision or a husband's will, but born of God. **John 1:12-13 (NIV)**

Topical Bibliography for the Quality Disciple

Spiritual Disciplines

1. Foster, Richard. 1988. *Celebration of discipline: the path to spiritual growth.* San Francisco, CA: Harper San Francisco.
2. Willard, Dallas. 1988. *The spirit of the disciplines: understanding how God changes lives.* San Francisco, CA: Harper San Francisco.

Prayer

3. Foster, Richard. 1992. P*rayer: Finding the Heart's True Home.* San Francisco, CA: Harper San Francisco.
4. Lockyer, Herbert. 1959. *All the prayers of the Bible.* Grand Rapids, MI: Zondervan.
5. Murray, Andrew. 1983, reprint. *Living a prayerful life.* Minneapolis, MN: Bethany House.
6. Duewel, Wesley L. 1986. *Touch the world through prayer.* Grand Rapids, MI: Francis Asbury Press.
7. Bounds, E. M. 2004. *The complete works of E. M. Bounds on prayer.* Grand Rapids, MI: Baker Books.
8. Sanders, J. Oswald. 1980. *Spiritual leadership.* Chicago, IL: Moody Press.

Bible Study

9. McKnight, Scot. 2008. *The blue parakeet: rethinking how you read the Bible.* Grand Rapids, MI: Zondervan.
10. McQuilkin, Robertson. 1992. *Understanding and applying the Bible*, Chicago, IL: Moody Press.
11. Peterson, Eugene H. 2006. *Eat this book: a conversation in the art of spiritual reading.* Grand Rapids, MI: Wm. B. Eerdmans Publishing Co.

Worship

12. MacDonald, James. 2006. *Downpour.* Nashville, TN: Broadman & Holdman.

13. Thomas, Gary. 2000. *Sacred Pathways: discover your soul's path to God, first Zondervan edition.* Grand Rapids, MI: Zondervan.

Grace
14. Strombeck, J. F. 1947, (2nd edition). *Disciplined by grace: studies in Christian conduct.* Moline, IL. Strombeck Agency, Inc; distributed by Van Kampen Press, Chicago, IL.
15. Swindoll, Charles, R. 2003. *The Grace Awakening.* Nashville, TN: W Publishing Group.

Community
16. Bates, Denny. 2005. *Building a Christian community of friends.* Florence, SC: Something New Christian Publishers.
17. Crabb, Larry. 1999. *The safest place on earth: where people connect and are forever changed.* Nashville, TN: Word Publishing.

Service
18. Rees, Erik. 2006. *S.H.A.P.E.: finding and fulfilling your unique purpose for life.* Grand Rapids, MI: Zondervan.

Evangelism
19. Coleman, Robert E. 1963, 1964, 1993. [New Spire edition 1994]. *The master plan of evangelism.* Grand Rapids, MI: Fleming H. Revell.
20. McQuilkin, Robertson. 1984, 2002 (rev). *The great omission.* Waynesboro, GA: Authentic Media.
21. Pippert, Rebecca Manley. 1979. *Out of the salt shaker and into the world.* Downers Grove, IL: InterVarsity Press.

Discipleship and the Christian Life
22. Allender, Dan B. 2006. *Leading with a limp: turning your struggles into strengths.* Colorado Springs, CO: Waterbrook Press.

23. Anderson, Keith R. and Reese, Randy D. 1999. *Spiritual mentoring: a guide for seeking and giving direction.* Downers Grove, IL: InterVarsity Press.

24. Arn, Win and Charles. 1998. *The master's plan for making disciples, 2nd edition.* Grand Rapids, MI: Baker Books.

25. Barna, George. 2001. *Growing true disciples: new strategies for producing genuine followers of Christ.* Colorado Springs, CO: Waterbrook Press.

26. Biehl, Bobb. 1996. *Mentoring: confidence in finding a mentor and becoming one.* Nashville, TN: Broadman and Holman Publishers.

27. Blackaby, Henry and Richard. 2001. *Spiritual leadership: moving people to God's agenda.* Nashville, TN: Broadman & Holman Publishers.

28. Boa, Kenneth. 2006. *The perfect leader: practicing the leadership traits of God.* Colorado Springs, CO: Victor (Cook Communications Ministries).

29. Burchett, Harold E. 1980. *Spiritual Life Studies.* Published by the author.

30. Campbell, James R. 2009. *Mentor like Jesus.* Nashville, TN: B & H Publishing Group.

31. Chambers, Oswald. 1985. *Christian disciplines: volumes 1 and 2.* Grand Rapids, MI: Chosen Books.

32. Chan, Simon. 1998. *Spiritual theology: a systematic theology of the Christian life.* Downers Grove, IL: InterVarsity Press.

33. Clinton, J. Robert and Richard W. 1991. *The mentor handbook.* Altadena, CA: Barnabas Publishers.

34. Cloud, Henry and Townsend, John. 2001. *How people grow: what the Bible reveals about personal growth.* Grand Rapids, MI: Zondervan.

35. Coleman, Robert E. 1987. *The Master Plan of Discipleship.* Old Tappan, NJ: Fleming H. Revell.

36. Hagberg, Janet O., and Guelich, Robert A. 2005, 1995. *The critical journey: stages in the life of faith.* Salem, WI: Sheffield Publishing Company.

37. Hanks, Billie Jr., and Shell, William A. 1982. *Discipleship: the best writings from the most experienced disciplemakers.* Grand Rapids, MI: The Zondervan Corporation.
38. Harney, Kevin. 2007. *Leadership from the inside out: examining the inner life of a healthy church leader.* Grand Rapids, MI: Zondervan.
39. Hart, Arcihbald D. 1995. *Adrenaline and Stress.* Nashville, TN: W. Publishing Group.
40. Hawkins, Greg L., Parkinson, Cally, and Arnson, Eric. 2007. *Reveal.* Barrington, IL: Willow Creek Resources.
41. Hawkins, Greg L. and Parkinson, Cally. 2008. *Follow me.* Barrington, IL: Willow Creek Resources.
42. Hendricks, Howard and William. 1995. *As iron sharpens iron.* Chicago, IL: Moody Publishers.
43. Hettinga, Jan David. 1996. *Follow me: experience the loving leadership of Jesus.* Colorado Springs, CO: NavPress.
44. Hull, Bill. 2004. *Choose the life: exploring a faith that embraces discipleship.* Grand Rapids, MI: Baker Books.
45. Hull, Bill. 1990. *The disciple-making church.* Grand Rapids, MI: Fleming H. Revell.
46. Hull, Bill. 1995. *Building high commitment in a low commitment world.* Grand Rapids, MI: Fleming H. Revell.
47. Hull, Robert W. 2006. *The complete book of discipleship.* Colorado Springs. NavPress.
48. Ingram, Chip. 2007. *Good to great in God's eyes: 10 practices great Christians have in common.* Grand Rapids, MI: Baker Books.
49. Lovelace, Richard J. 1985. *Renewal as a way of life: a guidebook for spiritual growth.* Downers Grove, IL: InterVarsity Press.
50. MacArthur, John F. Jr. 1976. *Keys to spiritual growth.* Old Tappan, NJ: Fleming H. Revell Company.
51. Mancini, Will. 2008. *Church unique: how missional leaders cast vision, capture culture, and create movement.* San

Francisco, CA: Jossey-Bass.

52. Maxwell, John C. 2005. *The 360-degree leader: developing your influence from anywhere in the organization.* Nashville, TN: Thomas Nelson, Inc.

53. McCallum, Dennis and Lowery, Jessica. 2006. *Organic disciplemaking: mentoring others into spiritual maturity and leadership.* Houston, TX: Touch Publications.

54. McIntosh, Gary L. and Rima, Samuel D., Sr. 1997. *Overcoming the dark side of leadership: the paradox of personal dysfunction.* Grand Rapids, MI: Baker Books.

55. Morley, Patrick, David Delk, and Brett Clemmer. 2006. *No man left behind: how to build a thriving disciple-making ministry for every man in your church.* Chicago, IL: Moody Publishers.

56. Nouwen, Henri J. M. 1975. *Reaching Out: the three movements of the spiritual life.* Garden City, NY: Doubleday and Company, Inc.

57. Ogden, Greg. 2003. *Transforming discipleship: making disciples a few at a time.* Downers Grove, IL: InterVarsity Press.

58. Olson, David T. 2008. *The American church in crisis.* Grand Rapids, MI: Zondervan.

59. Peterson, Jim. 1993. *Lifestyle discipleship: the challenge of following Jesus in today's world.* Colorado Springs, CO: NavPress.

60. Pue, Carson. 2005. *Mentoring leaders: wisdom for developing character, calling, and competency.* Grand Rapids, MI: Baker Books.

61. Putnam, David. 2008. *Breaking the discipleship code.* Nashville, TN: B&H Publishing Group.

62. Sanders, J. Oswald. (1994). *Spiritual discipleship.* Chicago, IL: Moody Publishers.

63. Scazzero, Peter L. (2003). *The emotionally healthy church: a strategy for discipleship that actually changes lives.* Grand Rapids, MI: Zondervan.

64. Stanford, Miles J. 1982. *The green letters: principles of spiritual growth.* Grand Rapids, MI: Zondervan Publishing House.

65. Stanley, Paul D. and Clinton, Robert J. 1992. *Connecting: the mentoring relationships you need to succeed in life.* Colorado Springs, CO: NavPress.

66. Waggoner, Brad J. 2008. *The shape of faith to come: spiritual formation and the future of discipleship.* Nashville, TN: B&H Publishing Group.

67. Willard, Dallas. 1998. *The divine conspiracy: rediscovering our hidden life in God.* San Francisco, CA: HarperSanFrancisco.

68. Willard, Dallas. 2006. *The great omission: reclaiming Jesus's essential teachings on discipleship.* San Francisco, CA: HarperSanFrancisco.

69. Warren, Rick. 1995. *The purpose-driven church.* Grand Rapids, MI: Zondervan.

70. Warren, Rick. 2002. *The purpose-driven life.* Grand Rapids, MI: Zondervan.

71. Wilkins, Michael J. 1992. *Following the Master: discipleship in the steps of Jesus.* Grand Rapids, MI: Zondervan Publishing House.

Books on workplace bullying, spiritual abuse, and moving on to new beginnings

There are an abundance of excellent resources on these topics. I've selected a few of the books from my own leadership library that I have found to be very helpful.

Namie, Gary & Ruth. 2009. *The bully at work: what you can do to stop the hurt and reclaim your dignity on the job.* Naperville, IN: Sourcebooks, Inc.

Johnson, David & Van Vonderen, Jeff. 1991. *The subtle power of spiritual abuse.* Bloomington, MN: Bethany House Publishers.

Cloud, Henry. 2010. *Necessary endings.* New York, NY: HarperCollins.

Foyle, Marjory. 2001. *Honorably wounded: stress among Christian workers.* Grand Rapids, MI: Kregel Publications.

Arterburn, Stephen & Felton, Jack. 1991. *Toxic faith: understanding and overcoming religious addiction.* Nashville, TN: Thomas Nelson.

Enroth, Ronald. 1993. *Churches that abuse.* 1993. Grand Rapids, MI: Zondervan.

Enroth, Ronald. *Recovering from churches that abuse.* 1994. Grand Rapids, MI: Zondervan.

Essential Spiritual Growth Resources from Something New Christian Publishers and Quality Leadership Consultants

Websites, Newsletter, and Blogs:

www.dennybates.com is the hub for all of our teaching and coaching resources. Check out our free downloads as well as our store.

www.thequalitydisciple.com links to dennybates.com.

www.qualityleadershipconsultants.com links to dennybates.com.

www.thequalitydisciple.blogspot.com is the teaching blog for Psalms of Discipleship.

www.facebook.com/denny.bates is my portal to social networking.

Dr. Denny Bates and Quality Leadership Tips For You is my newsletter. Featured leadership articles, devotional thoughts, and a menu of coaching and book resources.

Sign up at http://www.dennybates.com/#!contact/c3kh

You can follow me on Twitter @dennybates

Books:

Other titles from the Quality Discipleship Series:
- ❖ Passing It On…How To Make A *Quality* Disciple (E-Book only)
- ❖ How To Study And Apply The Bible To Your Life (E-Book only)
- ❖ Growing Up…Practical Bible Studies For New And Growing Christians (E-Book only)

❖ Building A Christian Community Of Friends (E-Book or printed copy)

❖ Psalms of Discipleship: Growing in Grace (E-Book or printed copy)

❖ Christmas Meditations of Worship: Four Weeks of Advent (E-Book or printed copy)

❖ Winter 2013: Living Above The Fray: Learning The Seven Healthy Leadership Principles That Will Shelter You From The Destructive Effects Of Leader-I-Tis

Retreat Journals:

❖ The Power – Broker's Guide To The Kingdom

❖ Four Legacies For A Life Change

❖ Three Commitments That Change A Life

❖ Growing In Grace: A Fresh Look At Biblical Discipleship

❖ Adding Quality To Your Life

Contact us for availability and cost.

www.dennybates.com/resouces

QUALITY LEADERSHIP CONSULTANTS

PROFESSIONAL COACHING, CONSULTING, AND TEACHING

Presenting Quality Ideas;
Producing Quality Leaders

Introducing Dr. Denny Bates

Professional Life, Business Coach, Teacher, Writer, Speaker And Consultant

DR. DENNY BATES
LEADING WITH QUALITY IN MIND

Why is it important for you to have a professional life coach and leadership trainer?

It has been said, "Experience is the best guide in life." The truth is *guided experience* is the best guide! Time, money, and emotional energy can be saved by linking up with a person who already understands where you are, where you want to go and has a good grasp on how to lead you there in a positive way.

What kind of guided experience do I offer?

Seasoned in both the market place and non-profit settings, I can offer you and/or your organization Quality Leadership coaching tracks with a relational emphasis. For instance, Personal Growth, Communication Skills, Building Healthy Relationships, Career Counseling / Job Performance, Life Transitions, Organizational Health; and for faith-based individuals and/or organizations, Spiritual Growth. My practical experience in both for-profit and non-profit settings, coupled with my academic and professional training, affords me the ability to offer you unique Quality Leadership services.

The JOHN MAXWELL **Team**

AN INDEPENDENT CERTIFIED COACH, TEACHER AND SPEAKER
WITH THE JOHN MAXWELL TEAM

My friend John Maxwell says,

"Everything rises and falls on leadership"

As a Leadership Specialist, I can help YOU in the marketplace!

✓ With years of experience working as a manager in the marketplace, I know what it takes to create a healthy organization. I can train your leaders and employees in effective teamwork and communication.

✓ I know how to help business leaders practice the kind of self-care that not only benefits them personally, but also adds value to the company.

✓ I know how to help a management team build a culture that places great value on integrity and success.

✓ I can help you and your leaders set reasonable goals and show you the tools to help you reach each one.

✓ I can help you reproduce your values, vision and passion in the lives of others.

✓ I can help you sharpen your leadership skills in a group coaching setting or one to one. As a professional life coach and leadership trainer, I can offer you the finest coaching and training resources available today as a certified coach, teacher and speaker for the John Maxwell Team.

Email dennybates@gmail.com

www.dennybates.com

What does a Disciple-Making Ministry look like?
It looks like . . .

SOMETHING *new*

"Do not call to mind the former things, or ponder things of the past; Behold, I will do something new . . ." Isaiah 43:18, 19a

- Is a ministry that focuses upon making Quality disciples for Jesus

- Is a ministry that encourages believers to connect in community and experience the discipled life

- Is a ministry that seeks to help other body of believers to learn how to live the discipled life through seminars, workshops, keynote speaking and interactive coaching

- Is a ministry where financial donations are not invested in buildings but where donations are invested in building lives

Contact Dr. Denny Bates for more information on how you and your church can create a culture of DiscipleMakers4Jesus

www.TheQualityDisciple.com

181

What Others Are Saying About My Leadership Coaching And Discipleship Via DiscipleMakers4Jesus (DM4J)

*I know and have worked with Denny Bates for more than a decade. Denny now serves as a leadership trainer and coach. It is my pleasure to recommend Denny as a valuable and trusted resource for leadership training and coaching. In addition to earning his doctoral degree in leadership, Denny is also an independent certified coach, teacher, and speaker for The John Maxwell Team. I believe you and your organization will benefit from his knowledge of what leaders need in order to grow as a leader. You will appreciate Denny's relational approach to leadership training and his ability to connect with people. Dr. Bates offers workshops, seminars, keynote speaking, and coaching ... aiding your personal and professional growth through study and practical application of John Maxwell's leadership methods. (**President and CEO of Regional Hospital**)*

Just wanted to let you know how much our time of coaching and leadership development has meant to me. Every time I am faced with a challenge I try to walk thru the Grace tree of wisdom. You set the example every day of the man of God I want to be. Thank you! (**Corporate Manager of Medical Services**)

*[I've learned] to keep the main thing the main thing!! To take care of the people that God puts in front of me everyday. (**Sales Manager of automotive dealership**)*

*Denny has been my friend, pastor, colleague, mentor and confidant for almost 10 years. During this time, Denny has led me through tough waters, given me wise counsel and taught me practical ways to live out my faith while falling more in love with my Savior. (**Youth Pastor**)*

Other than my own father, Denny has been my most trusted friend and spiritual mentor. Denny's discipleship has been truly transforming and helped me to realize the importance of investing in others as he has invested in me. **(Medical Device Consultant)**

I treasure my relationship with Denny because we share a common heart to help people discover all that Christ wants to do in and through them. **(Disciple-Making Missionary to Eastern Europe)**

I have known Denny for many years and have had the privilege to work with him on the same pastoral staff for over 5 years. During that time I have sought Denny's counsel on many issues ranging from personal struggles to theological questions. Denny has always provided me with poignant, gracious and thoughtful counsel. They say that everyone should have a mentor and I am blessed to be able to consider Denny my mentor. He has been an invaluable asset in my life and ministry. **(Clinical Counselor)**

My relationship with Denny has been personal, honest, and Christ-centered. Denny's common sense approach to the issues of life is always soundly based on scriptural principles. I remember discussing with Denny how I felt that I needed to do so much service for the Lord because of all the times I had failed Him. Denny gently said to me, "It's all about grace". I was reminded that there is no 'payback' plan for the Lord. **(Pastor)**

Having a group of peers who candidly discuss the awesome responsibility that each carries as a servant and hearing how God has responded so richly to our needs clearly demonstrates how marvelous is our God, who works in each of our lives to do His will. **(Hospital Vice-President in a discipleship group for executives)**

Denny and I have know each other for nearly fifteen years, we bonded shortly after he had his heart attack because of an illness I had years prior – Guillain-Barre Syndrome – that made me more aware of the right priorities I should have in life. Through this episode and having

183

children similar in age we bonded in a unique and special way rarely achieved between men. Approximately one year ago I lost my job as a senior executive at a large international company that I had been with 26 years, during the transition period of me finding another job Denny was an extreme encouragement to me. During a time when I was wrestling between accepting a position or not and I will never forget what Denny told me "You can just accept it as God's providential care". He was right! I later humbly accepted the position as President & Chief Operating Officer for a Subsea Oilfield Manufacturing company. **(Corporate Executive)**

Denny has been a teacher / mentor / discipler / encourager / prayer partner and great friend who God has used to help me keep a godly perspective on the different times & issues of life I've gone through as I've seek to follow Jesus. Once while praying with Denny through a career move, he encouraged me to think of the gifts & skills I had and then ask what I had a passion for, and then to ask God to show me how they can fit together. From this I learned to stop putting these gifts & skills in a "Box" and limiting what God could do with them, and use them for. For the first time, as I now work for a non-profit Christian organization as a warehouse manager, I feel I'm using the gifts and abilities God has given me to fulfill His purpose at something I really have a passion for! **(Former market place worker, now Missionary who is impacting the world)**

Denny met with me at 7 a.m. every Friday for a year. He came to me knowing he would receive my weekly burdens. This is not the way any of us would choose to begin our day. He does not judge nor do I ever feel judged. He is one of the most selfless and giving person I have ever met. This is easy to say because I know he is just a man. His obedience to God sets him apart. He taught me to live by grace, be long suffering, and love my wife regardless of my excuses. **(Medical Worker, Physical therapist assistant)**

Through a lifestyle of disciple making, Denny Bates has shown me what it truly means to live out Matthew 28: 19, 20. **(Educator)**

I've heard it said that on this side of eternity that there are only two things that you can be certain of: death and taxes. I'm certain of three things; the first two and that I have a friend in Denny Bates! I asked God at the beginning of my ministry to bring solid men into my life that would disciple me, teach me and hold me accountable. Denny has been an extreme answer to that prayer. **(Church-planting Pastor)**

Dr. Denny Bates opened my eyes to the power of small groups. He showed me what a true mentor really is. I will be forever grateful for his leadership, friendship, and love! **(Videographer)**

Practical application of God's teachings by normal, everyday family men such as myself; that's what DM4J means to me. Listening to and sharing the innumerable ways the Lord touches the lives of each and every man in this group is not only uplifting, but inspiring. From the greatest trials to what might seem trivial, God has a plan and a purpose for it all. The value of DM4J to me is immeasurable. **(Pharmacist)**

Praise For Living Above The Fray

"Denny has a tremendous heart for people, a very personal approach and a great desire to be a leader of men. Living Above The Fray is very much a case study for anyone who would be curious about the inner workings of a non profit organization and the challenges it presents." ~ Dennis D. Wells M.Min., M.A., LPC / Wellsprings Professional Counseling

"Denny [has] walked me through what it means to be a disciple. He taught me about mentoring, boundaries, and the richness of investing in others. This book can be beneficial to men and women who desire to lead through serving. Leadership skills are largely developed through experience. This book will provide leaders with an opportunity to reflect and go deeper. In our fast-paced society the importance of this practice is oftentimes disregarded, from our prayer time, to our parenting, to our relationship building, and unfortunately to our leadership development. Only when we slow down and take the time to see and seek wisdom in these areas do we experience true and lasting growth." ~ Erika Miller / M.S. Clinical Psychology

"I applaud you on publishing this book and truly trust that many, both leaders and followers, will benefit and be blessed by reading and following the 7 Leadership Principles as a package strongly founded on Scriptural principles." ~ Jack Walker / Founding Executive Director of Leadership Ministries Worldwide, Former Missionary Pilot and area director with Mission Aviation Fellowship

"This book provides an excellent how-to guide for overcoming our circumstances and becoming the kind of leaders who practice what we believe." ~ Dr. Lee Pearson / Director of Operations, SC Institute of Medicine and Public Health

"People are often unaware that they work in environments that are unhealthy, or they know the environment is unhealthy but can't understand exactly why. This book by Denny Bates clarifies so many of the issues and contrasts them with a healthy Biblical approach, giving readers the clarity and wisdom they need to deal with circumstances where they are or to know what to look for as they seek a healthier place to serve the Lord." ~ Stacey Severance / Worship Leader and Youth Pastor

"I have had the privilege of working with Denny for many years. Denny always amazed me at his insight and perspective in stressful and challenging situations. Denny has truly lived what he has written. I am thankful that I can call him a mentor. If anyone has ever lived what they have written about it is Denny Bates. I believe this book is best suited for anyone who finds themselves in a challenging relationship situation, whether it be personal or professional relationship." ~ Reeves Cannon, M.A., LPC, BCPCCC

"I have been reading Denny's books and blog for several years in addition to attending his teachings on leadership. His ability to communicate via the written word is extraordinary. He has a way of communicating that is second to none. He writes and teaches based on

his personal experience and lessons he has learned over a 30+ year career in both the private sector and the ministry." ~ Lamar Younginer B.S., M.S., / College Administrator

For Denny Bates" Living Above the Fray" is not just a book of words about life. It's the way he lives his life based on the Living word of Life, which he proclaims in every counseling session, every prayer, every encouragement for every one he meets and serves." ~ Dick Brown / President and CEO of Corporate Medical Services

"I have known Denny Bates for more than forty years. I have watched him, as have others, in order to study what a walk with Christ really looks like. Denny has set the bar high for the men around him...and he hasn't tried to do this...it is just who he is. Denny can be seen regularly at coffee shops and quiet corners mentoring men in their own walks with the Lord. I have seen Denny weather some tough storms that would have taken most men down with the ship, but his constant faith in the Lord he serves has allowed him to use those same storms to better equip and counsel other men, young and old, as they sit under his surgeon like discipling and training. I thank God for Dr. Denny Bates and the man that he has helped me become." ~ Wick Jackson / Sinner saved by Incredible Grace Husband Daddy Owner of Black Mountain Development Group Latin American Director of Envoy International

About Dr. Denny Bates

ABOUT THE AUTHOR: Dr. Denny Bates is Principal Consultant for Quality Leadership Consultants, Program Director of TrainingChurches.com, and a founding member of the John Maxwell Team of certified coaches, speakers, and trainers. He has earned degrees from Francis Marion College [B.S.], Columbia Biblical Seminary and School of Missions [MDiv, DMin]. With a doctoral degree in personal and organizational leadership, he is well equipped to serve as teacher, life coach, mentor, disciplemaker, motivational speaker and writer. Denny has written for an international publisher of Bible commentary, served as the Discipleship Pastor in the local church, as well as being as a leader in the marketplace. By God's grace, he seeks to live above the fray and "Press on!" Visit www.dennybates.com